FUN & FANTASY

Resource Guide

Edited by
Joanne Corker

Contributing Writers
Kathy Burdick

Marcia Fries

Kim Jordano

Gina Lems-Tardif

Project Directors
Carolea Williams

Rozanne Lanczak Williams

Art Director
Tom Cochrane

Designed by
Moonhee Pak

Illustrated by
Kathleen Dunne

Photographed by
Michael Jarrett

Special, heartfelt thanks to the many teachers and students across the country who have contributed their wonderful ideas and projects for this book.

TABLE OF CONTENTS

ACTIVITIES

LEVEL I

LEVEL II

INTRODUCTION

The *Learn to Read Resource Guide* provides a wealth of ideas and activities for using the *Fun & Fantasy* emergent reader series in a balanced literacy program. The *Fun & Fantasy* series includes 24 books that have been carefully developed to provide emergent readers with text they can successfully read on their own.

Children learn to read by reading and to write by writing. They develop skills, strategies, and fluency in a language-rich environment where they have many, varied opportunities to read, write, listen, and speak. The activities and ideas in this guide will provide you with a wide variety of motivational activities and innovative ideas for developing the literacy skills of emergent readers.

- games
- cooking
- pocket chart activities
- story murals
- graphing
- flannel board stories

Children who think of themselves as readers and writers, and whose every attempt is encouraged and supported, develop the confidence to take on new reading and writing challenges. We hope this guide will help you create a learning environment where children not only learn *how* to read but grow to *love* reading as well.

The ideas and projects were created by kindergarten, first- and second-grade teachers and their students all across the country. Their projects are photographed throughout the guide and include:

- text innovations
- class books
- individual student books
- story dramatizations
- oral reports
- puppets

RESOURCE GUIDE COMPONENTS

For each of the 24 books in the *Fun & Fantasy* series, there are three pages of information and extension activities. Each three-page section includes the following special features:

WRITING FRAMES

In this section, several writing frames modeling patterned language in the book are listed. For more information about using writing frames, see page 8.

MATERIALS

Easy-to-find materials are listed for each activity. Items common to all classrooms, such as scissors, crayons, and glue, are listed as art supplies. Collage materials include buttons, confetti, fabric and paper scraps, wiggly eyes, pipe cleaners, stickers, yarn, glitter, sequins, and dried macaroni.

SYNOPSIS

A short sentence and two-page book spread serve as a reminder of the book's content.

LEARNING A SKILL

One skill from the Related Skills list is developed for the book. Look at the great ideas in this section for ways to incorporate specific skill instruction.

RELATED SKILLS

Opportunities abound for teaching specific skills and reading strategies within the context of the series. Look at this section when planning instruction and addressing children's reading difficulties. For more information about related skills, see page 7.

ACTIVITIES

Unique and creative activities to extend learning make up this section. Projects include student-made big books, individual student books, murals, pocket chart activities, wall stories, and more.

PHOTOGRAPHS

A picture is worth a thousand words. Bright, colorful photographs of projects created by K–2 students appear throughout this guide and provide extra clarity to written directions.

LITERATURE LINKS

This section includes a list of books related to the themes and content of the *Learn to Read* series and the activities presented in this guide.

LINKING SCHOOL TO HOME

These take-home activities provide a non-threatening invitation to parents to become part of the classroom community. They encourage communication between home and school, help children connect home and school learning, and provide lots of opportunities for children to share and reinforce new skills.

ABOUT THE *LEARN TO READ FUN & FANTASY* SERIES

The *Learn to Read Fun & Fantasy* series is designed as a flexible resource for your early literacy program. The books have been written and carefully developed to provide emergent readers with text they can successfully read on their own. The engaging stories, along with colorful and appealing illustrations, make reading a fun and enjoyable experience.

The *Learn to Read Fun & Fantasy* series consists of 24 student-sized books for emergent readers and 24 matching big books. The books cover themes and topics young children love, such as bears, frogs, mice, and mudpies. The books are written on two levels:

Level I books contain eight pages of easy-to-read text. Usually one line of text appears on each page. There is one language pattern with no more than two changes on each page.

Level II books contain sixteen pages of slightly more difficult text. One or two lines of text appear on each page. The language pattern may change once throughout the story but remains highly repetitive.

The following special features in the *Learn to Read* series give maximum support to the beginning reader:

- Repetitive, predictable story lines provide instant success.

- Engaging stories with satisfying endings promote reading for meaning, rather than just sounding out words.

- Colorful illustrations in a variety of artistic styles closely match the text and provide added support.

- Large print is clear and well-placed.

- Natural language patterns (what the reader is used to hearing) move the reader easily through the text.

- Easy and fun activities on the inside back cover extend language learning.

BUILDING A BALANCED LITERACY PROGRAM

 Focusing on Skills and Strategies

The development of skills and strategies is an ongoing part of a balanced literacy program and occurs within the context of the reading and writing children are doing in the classroom. Skills can be taught formally when children are experiencing specific difficulties or when you anticipate difficulty with a particular text. Skills are tools learners use to make sense of a story when they read and to communicate effectively when they write. Most importantly, skills become strategies when learners apply them to solve their reading and writing difficulties. Developing strategies should be the focus of all skill instruction.

The components of a balanced literacy program include:

- reading aloud
- shared reading
- guided reading
- independent reading
- writing aloud
- shared writing
- guided writing
- independent writing

 Reading

READING ALOUD

Reading aloud is an important part of a balanced literacy program. Read to children several times a day in the classroom, and encourage parents to spend at least fifteen minutes a day reading to their children at home. Reading aloud makes a significant impact on the developing reading skills of young children. It builds comprehension, vocabulary, and listening skills, and exposes children to good literature written on a level higher than their instructional level.

Throughout this guide, Literature Links provide lists of books related to the theme and content of those in the series. Enrich your program by choosing read-aloud titles that extend student learning. For example, by reading aloud several versions of *City Mouse and Country Mouse*, you acquaint children with the story, supply background knowledge, and introduce important vocabulary. This introduction will help the child independently read the version of the book matched to his or her instructional level.

GUIDED READING

During guided reading, work with small groups of children who each have a copy of the same book. Children could also read small photocopies of a big book from a prior shared reading session. A guided reading session is a good time to model and reinforce emergent-level strategies such as one-to-one correspondence, return sweep, locating known and unknown words, letter/sound correspondence (phonics), context clues, and visual searching.

As children develop fluency, give them a book they haven't read before that matches their instructional level. Have each child work through the text while getting your and other readers' support. Children discuss the strategies that help them solve reading problems. This is where the real work of reading occurs. After several successful readings of the book, children can take the book home to read to parents.

SHARED READING

Shared reading is a powerful tool for teaching children what reading is all about. Children at all developmental levels are invited to join in the reading of a big book, poem, chant, or pocket chart story. Print is enlarged on shared reading material in order to encourage participation by the whole group. Modeling and child participation occur simultaneously. The emphasis during these sessions is on the joy and satisfaction of reading.

Big books in the *Learn to Read* series are designed primarily for shared reading with emergent readers. Use the repetition, rhyme, and predictable sentence patterns in the text, along with the strong support from illustrations, to lead beginning readers through successful reading experiences. Children enjoy reading the big books again and again during shared reading, and become favorite choices during independent reading.

Use previously-read big books for specific skill instruction. For example, *How to Make a Mudpie* is a great book to teach sequencing and the high-frequency words *you* and *need*. Or use *The Giraffe Made Her Laugh* to practice rhyming words.

INDEPENDENT READING

Emergent readers need many opportunities to read independently. Create a print-rich, reader-friendly classroom by making the following materials accessible:

- big books from previous shared reading sessions
- little books mastered during guided reading
- student-created books modeled after shared big books
- previously introduced pocket chart sets
- wall stories, story murals, and poetry charts
- trade books with text suitable for emergent readers

 *Writing*

Reading and writing are inseparable in a balanced literacy program. They are mutually supportive processes—growing expertise in one area influences the other. Encourage emergent readers to write through writing aloud, and shared, guided, and independent writing sessions.

WRITING ALOUD

Write on a chalkboard or chart in front of children and "think aloud" about the text as you write. This provides a powerful model on how to write, and exposes children to writing conventions such as spacing, punctuation, and spelling. Many teachers write the morning message "aloud" (a brief description of what's happening in the classroom or other noteworthy events).

SHARED WRITING

During a shared writing session, children write with you—it is a collaborative effort. As you guide the process, children supply ideas and input. Children at all developmental levels are invited to participate. Shared writing is a good time to write original stories, poems, class news, information books, or about shared experiences such as guest speakers or field trips. Use shared writing to create innovations and retellings of books children enjoyed during shared reading. For frames relating to specific book titles, refer to Writing Frames sections in this guide.

GUIDED WRITING

During a guided writing session, the child does the writing, while receiving your and other children's support and guidance. This is where the real work of writing occurs. On the emergent level, the guided writing session may be fairly structured. For example, group members could repeat and write the same sentence of a writing frame. You may comment on what the writers are doing correctly and supply missing elements to complete the sentence.

INDEPENDENT WRITING

A language-rich environment is not complete without lots of opportunities for children to write on their own. Encourage writing with journals, reading response logs, dramatic play centers with writing supplies, classroom mailboxes, student writing boxes, and observation journals in the science center. The simple text and patterned language in *Learn to Read* books provide a secure and inviting framework for children's written responses. After they read the books, some children will spontaneously adopt the language pattern and write their own versions.

RECOMMENDED READING FOR TEACHERS

Bialostok, Steve. *Raising Readers*. Peguis, 1992.

Fisher, Bobbi. *Thinking and Learning Together: Curriculum and Community in a Primary Classroom*. Heinemann, 1995.

Raymond, Allen (publisher). *Teaching K–8: Professional Magazine for Teachers*. Early Years, Inc.

Routman, Regie. *Invitations: Changing as Teachers and Learners*. Heinemann, 1991.

THE BEAR WENT OVER THE MOUNTAIN

Follow the bear on his way home in this
fun adaptation of the traditional song.

WHERE DID THE BEAR GO?
Story map

A bright idea and project from Jennifer
Botenhagen and her kindergartners, Lu
Sutton School, Novato, California

Materials
- ✓ butcher paper
- ✓ construction paper
- ✓ sentence strips
- ✓ art supplies

Have children plan and make a story map about the bear's
journey. Some children can work on the background for each
location, others can write the sentences, and some can make
bears. They can also add paw print stamps to show the bear's
travels. Volunteers can point to the bear's location on the map as classmates read or
sing the words. Challenge children to create appropriate hand and arm movements
to accompany the song.

BEARS ON THE MOVE
Moveable bear pictures

Materials
- ✓ paper bears
- ✓ popsicle sticks
- ✓ construction paper
- ✓ art supplies

Have children fold a piece of construction
paper in half and cut a slit in the folded end
6" across, leaving about 1" on either end uncut.
Invite them to illustrate where the bear will go and complete
the frame. Children then tape their paper bear to a popsicle
stick, poke the bear through the slit at the top, and sing the song.

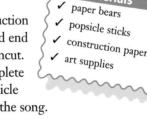

WRITING FRAMES

The bear _____ _____ the
_____.

To see what he could
see.

RELATED SKILLS

- correct usage: *went*
- parts of speech: *prepositions*
- phonics: *ee (see)*
- rhythm
- sequencing

BEAR BUTTER
Butter

Have children work in small groups to make Bear Butter. Fill baby food jars halfway with whipping cream, close the lids, and have children take turns shaking the jars to make butter. Children can stir honey into the butter and eat their treat with crackers.

Materials
✓ clean, empty baby food jars
✓ whipping cream
✓ honey
✓ plastic spoons and knives
✓ crackers

THE BEAR WENT OVER THE MOUNTAIN
Class storybook

Bright ideas and projects from Jennifer Botenhagen and her kindergartners, Lu Sutton School, Novato, California; and Marcia Fries and her multi-age class, Lee School, Los Alamitos, California

Materials
✓ drawing paper
✓ art supplies

Provide each child with blank pages for a class book. Brainstorm ideas for new places the bear might go, such as a bathtub or a store. Have children illustrate their ideas and print sentences about the bear picture. Compile pictures to make a class book with a colorful cover.

LEARNING A SKILL

Prepositional phrases

Make bear headbands using sentence strips with bear faces glued to the front. Brainstorm ideas for prepositional phrases to print on the headbands, such as "under the slide," "through the tunnel," and "around the sandbox." Have children wear their headbands outside on the playground as they perform the actions.

Materials
- ✓ sentence strips
- ✓ construction paper
- ✓ art supplies

LINKING SCHOOL TO HOME

Paper bag bear puppets

Send home materials for each child to make a paper bag bear puppet. Include construction paper, art supplies, and a brown paper bag. Provide parents with instructions to direct children where to take their puppet, such as under the chair, around the sofa, through the kitchen, into the living room, over the stool, and on the bed.

Materials
- ✓ small brown paper bags
- ✓ construction paper
- ✓ art supplies

LITERATURE LINKS

All About Where by Tana Hoban

Amy the Dancing Bear by Carly Simon

Bear by John Schoenherr

The Bear by Raymond Briggs

Bear Play by Miela Ford

Bears by Pascale De Bourgoing

Bear's Busy Year: A Book about Seasons by Marcia Leonard

How Do Bears Sleep? by E.J. Bird

Over, Under and Through by Tana Hoban

Red Bear by Bodel Rikys

Rosie's Walk by Pat Hutchins

We're Going on a Bear Hunt by Michael Rosen

HOW MANY?

The number of legs on an octopus, bug, kitten, and slug are explored in rhyme with questions and answers.

WRITING FRAMES

How many _____ on a _____?

_____ _____ on a _____?

RELATED SKILLS

• correct usage: *questions, a/an*

• numbers: *counting, one-to-one correspondence, words and numerals*

• punctuation: *capital letters, question marks*

• phonics: *rhyming words (bug/slug)*

𝒜 CTIVITY HOW MANY?

Class book of innovations

A bright idea and project from Karen Fuller and her pre-kindergartners, Mayflower School, Los Alamitos, California

Have each child dictate or write a "How many . . . ?" question and answer. Invite children to illustrate their questions and answers, and paste the printed statements beneath their pictures. Compile children's innovations into a book with a colorful cover for class sharing.

Materials
✓ 9" x 12" drawing paper
✓ sentence strips
✓ art supplies

Learn to Read Resource Guide • *Fun & Fantasy* Creative Teaching Press

$\mathcal{A}$ctivity WHAT ARE YOU WEARING?

Graphing and number mural

Count how many children in your class are wearing certain items of clothing such as sweaters, shorts, trousers, tennis shoes, dresses, and sandals. Help children place clothing cutouts on a graph and use the information to create a clothing mural entitled *How Many?* Children can trace paper doll patterns to make construction paper children and clothing and paste these on the mural with text printed beneath.

$\mathcal{A}$ctivity EDIBLE CRITTERS

Counting with fun snacks

Provide food items and toothpicks for children to create the following insects:

Crawly critters—banana slices, candy sprinkles, red candy "eyes," licorice "antennae"

Grasshoppers—celery, peanut butter, pretzel "legs," raisin "eyes"

Bugs—marshmallows, peanut butter, pretzel "legs," raisin "eyes"

Have children draw their creatures, and complete the sentence frames with numbers.

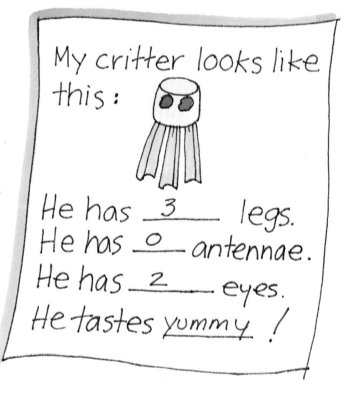

LEARNING A SKILL

Counting and one-to-one correspondence

Prestaple individual counting books with pages numbered one through eight. Have frames written on each page, concluding with "An ____ legged bug is a spider. Aahh!" On each page have children complete the sentence and draw a bug with an equal number of spots and legs.

Materials
- ✓ drawing paper
- ✓ art supplies

LINKING SCHOOL TO HOME

Counting books

Provide children with five-page booklets that have a question at the top of each page. The first page asks: "How many things have no legs?" and the second one asks: "How many things have one leg?" The number of legs increases by one on each page. Have children survey their home and on each page draw pictures of items that match the requirements. When children have filled the pages, encourage them to count the total number of items in their book and write that number on the last page.

Materials
- ✓ drawing paper
- ✓ art supplies

LITERATURE LINKS

Count! by Denise Fleming

Counting Kangaroos by Marcia Leonard

Counting Sheep by John Archambault

Counting Wildflowers by Bruce McMillan

Each Orange Had Eight Slices: A Counting Book by Paul Giganti

How Many Snails? A Counting Book by Paul Giganti, Jr.

One Ballerina Two by Vivian French

One Cow, Moo, Moo! by David Bennett

Ten Black Dots by Donald Crews

Up to Ten and Down Again by Lisa Campbell Ernst

What Comes in 2's, 3's, and 4's? by Suzanne Aker

Who's Counting? by Nancy Tafuri

HOW TO MAKE A MUDPIE

Find out the ingredients for a mudpie in this wonderful how-to book.

You need some dirt.   You need some water.

ACTIVITY

MINI ICE CREAM FLOATS
Individual interactive horizontal storybooks

A bright idea and project from Trisha Callella and her kindergartners, Rossmoor School, Los Alamitos, California

Provide each child with two strips of 6" x 18" white paper. Help children fold each strip to make four accordion-style pages and tape these together to form eight pages. Children can glue one sentence frame at the bottom of each page. Ask them to write "You" in the space for each sentence and draw an illustration on the page. Help children trace around the cup pattern to make the cover for their book. They can glue the "cup" to the front page and decorate the cover with a title and pictures. Help children tape cellophane over the cover, leaving the top open to insert a flexible drinking straw. They can use the drinking straw as a pointer as they read their story.

Materials

- ✓ 6" x 18" white paper strips
- ✓ copies of sentence frames with a blank for the word *you*
- ✓ construction paper
- ✓ cup pattern
- ✓ cellophane
- ✓ flexible drinking straws
- ✓ art supplies

WRITING FRAMES

To make a _____ you need _____.

How do you make a _____?

You _____.

RELATED SKILLS

- cooperating
- high-frequency words: *you, need*
- sequencing

HOW TO MAKE AN ICE CREAM FLOAT

Interactive wall storybook

A bright idea and project from Trisha Callella and her kindergartners, Rossmoor School, Los Alamitos, California

Materials

✓ butcher paper
✓ drawing paper
✓ construction paper
✓ tempera paint
✓ plastic zipper bags
✓ plastic spoons
✓ paper cups
✓ flexible drinking straws
✓ art supplies

Fold lengths of butcher paper to form an accordion-style book with 18" x 22" pages. Cut around the edges of the book to form a "cup" shape, leaving 10" joined at the side. Print the title *How to Make an Ice Cream Float*. Have children paint multi-colored ice cream scoops to paste on the bottom half of each page. Glue plastic bags to the top half of each page to hold items described in each sentence, such as flattened paper cups on one page and colored paper "ice cream scoops" on another. Conclude the book with the names and pictures of the children and the sentence: "You need some thirsty kids." Display the story so children can manipulate items as they read each page. Children can also remove contents from all the bags and correctly replace items on each page as they read the sentences.

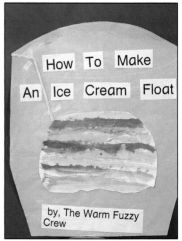

CREATIVE COOKBOOK

Recipes

Illustrate the importance of giving specific directions by asking children to explain how to make a peanut butter and jelly sandwich. Visually demonstrate each step as children give directions. For example, use fingers rather than a knife if the child says, *Spread peanut butter on the bread.* Have students write a recipe book for parents on how to cook favorite recipes. Ask adult volunteers to take exact dictation of these recipes for children to illustrate. Make copies of the class cookbook to give as gifts.

Materials

✓ sliced bread
✓ butter knife
✓ peanut butter
✓ jelly
✓ construction paper
✓ art supplies

LEARNING A SKILL

Verbs

Read *How Do You Make a Bubble?* and have children brainstorm ideas for "How do you ____?" questions.

Materials
- ✓ *How Do You Make a Bubble?* by William H. Hooks, Joanne Oppenheim, & Barbara Brenner
- ✓ drawing paper
- ✓ art supplies

Write each question and answer idea on a sheet of paper and have children use a verb to complete the answer. Invite children to illustrate their sentences for a class book of questions and answers.

LINKING SCHOOL TO HOME

Sandwich recipes

Encourage parents and children to create a super sandwich at home. Have children write their sandwich recipes on recipe cards, listing ingredients and directions, and drawing an illustration. Assemble student recipe cards to make a class book with a "sandwich" cover entitled *Super Sandwiches*. Choose one recipe each month and have volunteers bring in the ingredients to make the sandwiches.

Materials
- ✓ sandwich ingredients
- ✓ 8 1/2" x 11" recipe cards
- ✓ construction paper
- ✓ art supplies

Ketchup and cheese sandwich

ketchup
cheese
tomato
cucumber
lettuce
bread

Spread ketchup on bread. On the top of the ketchup put a piece of cheese, tomato, cucumber, and some lettuce. Put another slice of bread on top of the lettuce. Put your sandwich on the grill to toast the bread. Yum!

LITERATURE LINKS

Burger Stew by Susan Patron

The Cake That Mack Ate by Rose Robart

The High Rise Glorious Skittle Skat Roarious Sky Pie Angel Food Cake by Nancy Willard

How Do You Make a Bubble? by William H. Hooks, Joanne Oppenheim, and Barbara Brenner

How to Make a Book by Aliki

How to Make an Apple Pie and See the World by Marjorie Priceman

Mud by Wendy Cheyette Lewison

Oh My Baby Bear! by Audrey Wood

Peanut Butter and Jelly: A Play Rhyme by Nadine Westcott

Shazam! Simple Science Magic by Laurence B. White, Jr. and Ray Broekel

Thunder Cake by Patricia Polacco

I CAN READ

A young boy explores the world
of environmental print.

WRITING FRAMES

I can read _____.

I can read (<u>location words</u>).

RELATED SKILLS

- classifying

- high-frequency words:
  I, can, read

- vocabulary:
  environmental print

- parts of speech: *nouns*

- phonics: *ea*
  (read—present tense)

A ACTIVITY

A CLASS OF READERS
Three-dimensional mural

A bright idea and project from Tricia Callella and her kindergartners, Rossmoor School, Los Alamitos, California

Cut a large brown book shape from butcher paper and attach it to the wall. Have each child create a paper doll self-portrait from art supplies and collage materials. Help children make a mini "book" for their doll to hold. Paste dolls and books on the butcher paper to create a mural.

Materials

✓ brown butcher paper
✓ art supplies
✓ collage materials

WORLD OF PRINT
Word collage

Have children examine various resources to find and bring in words or phrases they can read. Attach the words to the bulletin board and supply a pointer so children can read the words they know.

Materials
- ✓ items with writing (cereal boxes, food wrappers, advertisements, newspapers)
- ✓ pointer

COMMUNITY READ
Guest reader

Participate in a school "Community Read-Aloud Day." Invite someone from the community to your class to read a book and discuss with children how and why reading is important in their lives.

Materials
- ✓ community reader
- ✓ book

KIDS CAN!
Mural and class book

A bright idea and project from Gerianne Smith and her kindergartners, Minnie Gant School, Long Beach, California

Take photographs of children performing activities in different environments. Use these pictures to create a class book entitled *Kids Can . . . .*

Materials
- ✓ camera
- ✓ construction paper
- ✓ art supplies

LEARNING A SKILL

High-frequency words

With your class, brainstorm a list of all the things children can do. Have each child use a paper plate to make a "face" book cover, adding yarn for hair and construction paper for facial features. Provide children with precut paper circles to write or dictate "I can ____" statements. Have them illustrate each page. Staple the circular pages inside the face covers to make books for class sharing.

Materials
- ✓ paper plates
- ✓ circles of writing paper (paper plate size)
- ✓ construction paper
- ✓ collage materials
- ✓ art supplies

LINKING SCHOOL TO HOME

Environmental print

A bright idea and project from Linda Benton and her first graders, Westwood School, Westwood, California

Have each child take home a sheet of paper with a space for his or her name and the sentence frame "I can read ____." Children can glue, tape, or draw a favorite word such as the name of a break-fast cereal, magazine, or toy on the sentence frame. Assemble pages with a colorful cover to make a class book of environmental print. Children can also make personal *I Can Read* books using environmental print.

Materials
- ✓ drawing paper
- ✓ environmental print
- ✓ art supplies
- ✓ construction paper

LITERATURE LINKS

The Bee Tree by Patricia Polacco

Herds of Words by Patricia MacCarthy

I Hate English! by Ellen Levine

I Hate to Read by Rita Marshall

I Like Books by Anthony Browne

I Read Signs by Tana Hoban

I Read Symbols by Tana Hoban

I Walk and Read by Tana Hoban

My Book by Ron Maris

Quick! Turn the Page! by James Stevenson

The Wednesday Surprise by Eve Bunting

When Will I Read? by Miriam Cohen

I CAN WRITE

A young girl celebrates her writing skills.

I can write on the sidewalk.   I can write on the paper.

WE CAN WRITE
Class photography book

A bright idea and project from Beth Ellis and her kindergartners, Hopkinson School, Los Alamitos, California

Materials
- ✓ 12" x 18" black construction paper
- ✓ 9" x 12" construction paper
- ✓ sentence strips
- ✓ camera
- ✓ art supplies

Make a class list of different writing surfaces and take photographs of children writing with partners on those places. Paste each photograph on 9" x 12" construction paper and glue it to a piece of black construction paper. Help children print a "We can write ____" statement on a sentence strip. Invite them to correctly match sentences and photographs by pasting each sentence strip on the appropriate page. On the last page print "We can write!" and show all the children's names. Compile pages to make a class big book.

WRITING FRAMES

I can write on ____.

I can write with a ____.

I can ____. We can ____.

RELATED SKILLS

- classifying
- high-frequency words: *I, can, write, on, the*
- parts of speech: *nouns, prepositions*
- phonics: *wr (write)*
- vocabulary: *compound words*

WRITING STATIONS
Writing media and materials

Materials
- ✓ variety of writing tools and materials

Set up writing stations with different writing tools for children to explore. Stations might include children dipping paintbrushes in water to write on cement; chalk in water to write on paper; feathers in black paint to write on paper; cotton swabs in paint to make dot letters.

WRITE ON!
Never-ending class story

Have children take turns writing a never-ending story roll about different kinds of writing. Invite each writer to use a different colored writing tool and continue the process until they fill the roll of paper with writing.

KIDS ON THE GO!
Wall chart

A bright idea and project from Gerianne Smith and her kindergartners, Minnie Gant School, Long Beach, California

Provide children with colored paper shapes and have them create self-characters performing an action (motor skill). Help children complete "I can _____" sentences to display near their characters.

LEARNING A SKILL

Publishing

Establish a class Publishing Center with materials and media for children to use to "publish" their stories. Invite adult volunteers and older children to assist at the center.

Materials
- ✓ writing paper
- ✓ construction paper (for covers)
- ✓ picture and alphabet letter stamps
- ✓ stamp pads
- ✓ stickers
- ✓ machines (computer, printer, typewriter)
- ✓ art supplies

LINKING SCHOOL TO HOME

Collage mini-book

Send home a six-page mini-book entitled *I Can Write*. Children can decorate the cover and paste a writing surface on each page, such as face tissue, typing paper, and thank-you cards. Beneath each sample have them complete the sentence "I can write on ____." Invite children to share their books with classmates.

Materials
- ✓ construction paper
- ✓ art supplies

LITERATURE LINKS

Arthur's Pen Pal by Lillian Hoban

Dear Peter Rabbit by Alma Flor Ada

Dear Zoo by Rod Campbell

I Can Write by Dr. Seuss

The Jolly Christmas Postman by Janet and Allan Ahlberg

The Jolly Postman by Janet and Allan Ahlberg

Look What I Can Do! by Jose Aruego

Lyle at the Office by Bernard Waber

The Signmaker's Assistant by Tedd Arnold

Stringbean's Trip to the Shining Sea by Vera Williams

LITTLE GREEN FROG

A fun-to-sing song about a hilarious little froggy.

WRITING FRAMES

"_____!" said the little green frog one day.

"_____!" said the little green frog.

"_____!" said the little green frog one day.

And his _____ went _____, _____, _____!

RELATED SKILLS

• parts of speech: *descriptive words (adjectives)*

• phonics: *ee/gr (green), fr (frog)*

• punctuation: *commas, exclamation points, quotation marks*

• vocabulary: *body parts, sound words (onomatopoeia)*

A c t i v i t y

FROG PEEK-OVERS
Individual shape books

A bright idea and project from Marne Busatto and her kindergartners, Markahm School, Mount Lebanon, Pennsylvania

Make a frog cover pattern from tagboard as shown. Help each child trace and cut out his or her own cover from green construction paper. Cut on the dotted lines only, poking scissors through the paper to cut under the frog's hands and chin. Staple sheets of writing paper to the bottom portion. Fold up on the fold line so the bottom portion tucks under the frog's hands and chin. Children can decorate the cover using art supplies and wiggly eyes. Invite children to write frog stories, their own version of *Little Green Frog*, or write and illustrate the frog's life cycle.

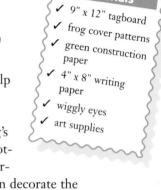

Materials
✓ 9" x 12" tagboard
✓ frog cover patterns
✓ green construction paper
✓ 4" x 8" writing paper
✓ wiggly eyes
✓ art supplies

FROGGY WORDS
Pocket chart and illustrated class book

A bright idea and project from Mary Kurth and her kindergartners, Black Earth School, Black Earth, Wisconsin

Write key story words on cards to display in a pocket chart. Read the story aloud and have children take turns pointing to the words and role playing the frog's actions. Print key words on construction paper and have children work in pairs to illustrate the words. Partners can show their picture as classmates read the words.

Materials
- ✓ word cards
- ✓ pocket chart
- ✓ 12" x 18" construction paper
- ✓ art supplies

GA-LUMP
Wall story

A bright idea and project from Kim Jordano and her kindergartners, Lee School, Los Alamitos, California

Materials
- ✓ sentence strips
- ✓ butcher paper
- ✓ tempera or watercolor paint
- ✓ art supplies

Have children paint a picture to illustrate the frog's actions for each sentence in the text. Glue pictures and sentences on butcher paper and have children dramatize the frog's actions as they read the mural.

LITTLE OR BIG?
Size comparisons

Place a picture of Little Green Frog between two "ponds" labeled *Big* and *Little*. Give children three minutes to find objects in the classroom that are bigger and smaller than the frog. Have them place the items in the correct "pond" and give reasons for their decision.

Materials
- ✓ two blue hula hoops or blue construction paper "ponds"
- ✓ *Little* and *Big* labels
- ✓ Little Green Frog picture or toy frog
- ✓ various classroom items

Activity

SPRINGY FROGS
Three-dimensional frogs

Give each child two halves of a paper plate, two halves of a foam ball, and four strips of green construction paper. Glue the curved edge of one plate half to the straight edge of the other half. Accordion-fold green strips and glue them to the bottom to make the frog's legs and arms. Attach ping-pong or foam balls as eyes and use a black marker to add irises and a mouth. Invite children to use their frogs when singing the rhyme.

Materials
- ✓ green paper plates (cut in half)
- ✓ green construction paper strips
- ✓ white ping-pong or foam balls (cut in half)
- ✓ black markers
- ✓ art supplies

LEARNING A SKILL

Sound words (onomatopoeia)

Read the following words to children: *pop, fizzle, drip, honk*. Explain that these words sound like the sound they make when vocalized. Have children write the words and draw a picture for each sound. Brainstorm other sound words children know. They can choose some of these words to write and illustrate.

Materials
- ✓ drawing paper
- ✓ art supplies

LINKING SCHOOL TO HOME

Home reading

As children read the book at home, have parents provide the sound effects and read the sound words. Children can pantomime the actions as parents read the story. Families might tape-record their presentations to share with the class.

LITERATURE LINKS

A Fly Went By by Mike McClintock

Amazing Frogs and Toads by Barry Clarke

Frog by Angela Royston

Frog and Toad Are Friends by Arnold Lobel

Frog and Toad Together by Arnold Lobel

Frog Odyssey by Juliet and Charles Snape

From Tadpole to Frog by Wendy Pfeffer

Jump, Frog, Jump! by Robert Kalin

Lily Pad Pond by Bianca Lavies

Pondlarker by Fred Gwynne

Seven Froggies Went to School by Kate Duke

Tuesday by David Wiesner

PIGS

Pigs star in this adaptation of the popular counting rhyme "One, Two, Buckle My Shoe"

PIGS!

Paper bag pig puppets

A bright idea and project from Kimri Vella and her first graders, Lee School, Los Alamitos, California

Help children trace around patterns to make one head and four limbs for each pig puppet. Have them place clothing patterns on colored paper to trace T-shirts, skirts, and trousers and decorate clothes with wrapping paper cutouts. After drawing a face on the pig, have each child glue it to the bottom flap of the paper bag. Attach limbs to the clothes and paste clothes on one side of the bag beneath the head. Glue the *Pigs* rhyme to the back of the puppet. Children can use pig puppets to recite the rhyme and tell their own pig stories for classmates.

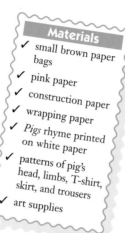

Materials
- ✓ small brown paper bags
- ✓ pink paper
- ✓ construction paper
- ✓ wrapping paper
- ✓ *Pigs* rhyme printed on white paper
- ✓ patterns of pig's head, limbs, T-shirt, skirt, and trousers
- ✓ art supplies

WRITING FRAMES

One pig on the _____,
Two pigs on the _____ . . .

RELATED SKILLS

- **numbers:** *counting, words and numerals*
- **phonics:** *rhyming words (four/door; six/sticks)*
- **punctuation:** *commas*
- **rhythm**

PLENTY OF PIGS

Pig masks

Provide children with two paper plates each. Have them cut one in half for ears and use a paper cup to trace two construction paper "eyes." Help children cut out the eyes and place the paper cup "snout" between them. Tape the cup and ears to the plate to complete the pig. Have groups of ten children work together to rewrite and act out their own story for the class with their masks.

Materials
- ✓ pink paper plates
- ✓ construction paper
- ✓ 3-oz. pink paper cups
- ✓ pencils
- ✓ elastic
- ✓ art supplies

ONE, TWO, BUCKLE MY SHOE

Story adaptations

Ask children if *Pigs* reminds them of another rhyme—"One, Two, Buckle My Shoe." Explain that when words from a rhyme or story are changed to make a similar story it is called an "adaptation." Invite children to make an adaptation using their favorite animals. Older children might create an adaptation to count backward.

Materials
- ✓ drawing paper
- ✓ art supplies

COUNTING ON PIGS

Number line

Space numbers evenly and glue them on the butcher paper, creating a number line. Give each child a sheet of pink paper to make two pigs. Have children cut out their pigs and glue the correct number of pigs above each numeral. Write each number word below the number line in a catchy rhyme for children to recite. Note: You need 55 pigs in all for this activity.

Materials
- ✓ butcher paper
- ✓ pink construction paper
- ✓ 12"-high construction paper numbers
- ✓ art supplies

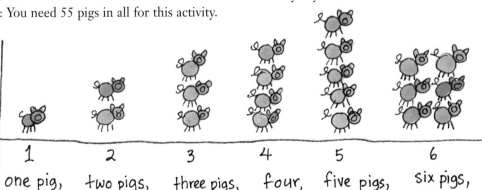

one pig, two pigs, three pigs, four, five pigs, six pigs, there are more . . .

LEARNING A SKILL

Counting forward and backward

Have children make an accordion-style number book using stickers, magazine pictures, and stamps to illustrate the number on each page. They can make their book count forward or backward and share their work with classmates.

Materials
- ✓ drawing paper
- ✓ stickers
- ✓ magazines
- ✓ stamps
- ✓ stamp pads
- ✓ art supplies

LINKING SCHOOL TO HOME

Counting and ordering numbers

Encourage families to go on a counting spree and count objects in their home. Children can count anything—spoons, pens, or toys. For example, they might count spoons on the counter, spoons in the sink, spoons in the dishwasher, spoons in the drawer, and spoons on the table. Parents can help children print each number and location on separate index cards and then put the cards in numerical order. Note: In most cases numbers will not be consecutive.

Materials
- ✓ index cards
- ✓ variety of household objects

LITERATURE LINKS

Animal Numbers by Bert Kitchen

Just One More by Michelle Koch

One Cow, Moo, Moo! by David Bennett

One Duck, Another Duck by Charlotte Pomerantz

One, Two, Three and Four: No More? by Catherine Gray

Pig Pig Gets a Job by David McPhail

Piggies by Don Wood and Audrey Wood

Pigs by Robert Munsch

Pigs from One to Ten by Arthur Geisert

Pigs in Hiding by Arlene Dubanevich

The Three Little Javelinas by Susan Lowell

The Three Little Pigs by Paul Galdone

RAIN

Rain falls in this adaptation of a favorite poem; illustrated with colorful cut paper.

WRITING FRAMES

Rain on the _____, rain on the _____.

Rain on the _____, but not on me!

RELATED SKILLS

• parts of speech: *prepositions*

• phonics: *ai (rain), ee (tree), rhyming words (tree, bee, me)*

• punctuation: *commas, exclamation points*

• vocabulary: *colors*

A c t i v i t y

NOT ON ME!
Class mural and wall story

A bright idea and project from Liz Newman and her kindergartners, Hidden Valley School, Santa Rosa, California

Use a rolling pin to cover butcher paper with watered-down tempera paint. Have children use corks and sponges to paint the tissue paper with tempera. When dry, children can cut the dry paper into small colored shapes and use liquid starch to paste the pieces onto their black umbrellas. Arrange completed umbrellas on the butcher paper, adding handles made from yarn. Ask children to draw themselves standing beneath their umbrellas next to someone else standing in the rain. Print each child's dictated sentence near his or her illustration. When the scene is dry, children can add white daubs of paint for "rain." Display lengths of butcher paper along the wall to form a story mural for children to reread with friends.

Materials

✓ butcher paper
✓ rolling pin
✓ flat pans
✓ precut black construction paper umbrellas (about 11" x 17")
✓ tempera paint
✓ corks
✓ sponges
✓ white tissue paper
✓ lengths of thick colored yarn
✓ liquid starch
✓ construction paper
✓ art supplies

Rain on the caterpillar. But not on me!

Diane

Learn to Read Resource Guide • *Fun & Fantasy*   Creative Teaching Press

RAIN!
Step books

A bright idea and project from Liz Newman and her kindergartners, Hidden Valley School, Santa Rosa, California

Make individual step books for children as follows:

Materials
- ✓ 8 1/2" x 11" white paper
- ✓ art supplies

1. Overlap three sheets of paper, leaving a 1" margin at the bottom of each page.

2. Hold the pages securely so they remain overlapped, and fold.

3. Staple through all layers next to the fold.

4. On each step, write a sentence from *Rain* to retell the story or the child's own innovation.

Invite children to draw a picture about each sentence above the text.

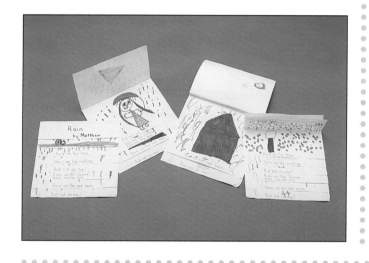

RAINY DAY WALK
Raindrop-shaped books

Wait for a rainy day to do this fun activity. Provide children with white raindrop-shaped cover pages and have them use markers to draw a picture of the outside environment. Place their cover pages outside the classroom to catch rain and become "rain paintings." It only takes a few seconds in the rain for the colors to run. Take a rainy day walk around the school and have children write about their experiences or dictate ideas on raindrop-shaped pages. Staple pages inside the raindrop cover for class sharing.

Materials
- ✓ precut raindrop-shaped books
- ✓ watercolor markers

Hint: If there is no rain, children can spray or spritz their pictures with water.

IT'S RAINING, IT'S POURING
Class book or paper collage

A bright idea and project from Kimri Vella and her first graders, Lee School, Los Alamitos, California

Materials
- ✓ construction paper
- ✓ art supplies

Rewrite the lyrics of *Rain* to create a class big book. Children can illustrate pages with construction paper scraps.

LEARNING A SKILL

Rhyming words

A bright idea and project from Renee Keeler and her first graders, Lee School, Los Alamitos, California

Model how to write a new verse for *Rain* using the name of a class pet or friend. Ask for volunteers who would like their names included in the new text. Write their names on the chalkboard. Brainstorm rhyming words for the children's names such as *hen* for *Ben*. Print new verses on construction paper for children to illustrate with crayon resist—drawing pictures with crayon and painting them with watercolor. Display completed artwork as a wall story or class book.

Materials
✓ construction paper
✓ watercolor paint
✓ art supplies

LINKING SCHOOL TO HOME

New verses

Send home sentence strips with the writing frame shown. Have children create and illustrate new verses using the names of their family members.

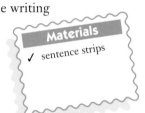

Materials
✓ sentence strips

LITERATURE LINKS

Amy Loves the Rain by Julia Hoban

Amy Loves the Snow by Julia Hoban

Amy Loves the Sun by Julia Hoban

Bringing the Rain to Kapiti Plain by Verna Aardema

Listen to the Rain by Bill Martin, Jr. and John Archambault

Rain by Robert Kalan

Red Day, Green Day by Edith Kunhardt

Roger's Umbrella by Daniel Pinkwater

Storm's Coming by Dave Saunders and Julie Saunders

Water's Way by Lisa Westberg Peters

Weather by Pascale de Bourgoing

What Will the Weather Be? by Lynda DeWitt

LEARNING A SKILL

Sequencing ideas

Help children make seven picture labels: *sky, tree, flower, grass, rock, soil,* and *worm.* Seven volunteers can each hold a picture to show the sequence in *Under the Sky* and then move so their pictures show a different sequence. Ask: *Can this book go in any order?* Have children illustrate index cards to show sequence ideas for other stories such as *Rosie's Walk.* Children can work in small groups to sequence story cards in a pocket chart.

> **Materials**
> ✓ construction paper strips
> ✓ pocket chart
> ✓ index cards
> ✓ *Rosie's Walk* by Pat Hutchins

LINKING SCHOOL TO HOME

Story frames

Provide each child with an "in the House" frame to take home and complete with his or her family. Children can decorate their house on the back side of the paper. Hint: Children might find it easier to start from the bottom of their house and work up to the roof; then they can read it from top to bottom.

> **Materials**
> ✓ "In the House" sentence frame

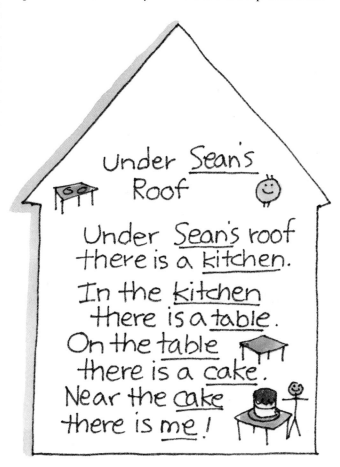

LITERATURE LINKS

Deep Down Underground by Olivier Dunrea

The Gift of the Tree by Alvin Tresselt

I Know an Old Lady by Nadine Westcott

Look Up, Look Down by Tana Hoban

The Magic Schoolbus Inside the Earth by Joanna Cole

Nature Walk by Douglas Florian

Rosie's Walk by Pat Hutchins

Sky Above, Earth Below by Joanna Cotler

The Tiny Seed by Eric Carle

The Tree by Judy Hindley

Under the Sun and Over the Moon by Kevin Crossley-Holland

What Joe Saw by Anna Grossnickle Hines

Why the Sky Is Far Away: A Nigerian Folktale by Mary Joan Gerson

WHAT DO YOU SEE?

Sequential counting of body parts comes together in one scary monster.

ACTIVITY

CREATURE FEATURE
Group monster art and stories

A bright idea from Marcia Smith, Lu Sutton School, Novato, California

Have children work in collaborative groups to create a silly monster. Each group member draws and cuts out one monster part such as its head, legs, arms, or body. Groups can also use magazine pictures to add features to their creatures. Have children paste their monsters on paper and use the sentence frames in the book to write about them.

Materials
✓ construction paper
✓ sentence strips
✓ magazines
✓ art supplies

I see two scary eyes, one scary mouth and ten scary teeth!

ACTIVITY

MONSTER MASH
Class snack

Before the activity have children draw and decorate their own monster place mats on white paper. Working together, write a class recipe for Monster Mash using foods such as cereal, dried fruit, nuts, crackers, and candies. Ask children to bring these foods to class in small plastic bags and mix the ingredients in a bowl. Pour the Monster Mash into small paper cups for children to sort on their monster place mats before enjoying the yummy treat.

Materials
✓ large bowl
✓ bite-sized foods
✓ small paper cups
✓ 8 1/2" x 11" white paper or blank place mats
✓ art supplies

MONSTER PARADE
Paper bag monsters

Cut out eyes and slits in the sides of grocery bags for children to wear on their heads. Children can decorate their bags with feathers, glitter, and construction paper to make monsters. Read *The Monster Book of ABC Sounds,* and have a monster parade through the school with children making monster sounds. Children can also name and write stories about their monsters to paste on the back of their monster paper bags.

Materials
✓ paper grocery bags
✓ feathers
✓ glitter
✓ construction paper
✓ art supplies
✓ *The Monster Book of ABC Sounds* by Alan Snow

EDIBLE MONSTERS
Fruit and vegetable monster sculptures

Have children bring in fresh fruit and vegetables to make monsters. Take photographs of each child's creation or have children draw their models for a class display. Have children use descriptive words as they write or dictate sentences describing their monsters. They also might like to eat tasty parts of their monster for a snack.

Materials
✓ fresh fruit and vegetables (cauliflower, bananas, peppers, carrots, apples, grapes)
✓ toothpicks
✓ paper plates
✓ camera
✓ drawing paper
✓ art supplies

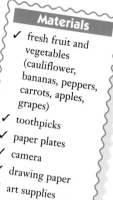

WHAT CAN MONSTERS DO?
Class book

A bright idea and project from Gerianne Smith and her kindergartners, Minnie Gant School, Long Beach, California

Materials
✓ construction paper
✓ art supplies

Reread *What Do You See?* with children. Talk about the scary monster on page eight and ask: *What can this monster do? What does it eat?* Model writing by printing children's ideas on the chalkboard. Have each child draw and decorate a scary monster on white construction paper and dictate a sentence about it for a class book.

LEARNING A SKILL

Counting

Provide children with monster picture sheets and at least 21 counters, pieces of cereal, or beans. Read the story and have children place the correct number of counters on their monster sheets. Challenge students to create their own monster number sentences for classmates to count.

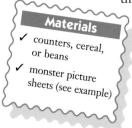

Materials
✓ counters, cereal, or beans
✓ monster picture sheets (see example)

LINKING SCHOOL TO HOME

Animal riddles

Send home a sheet entitled *What Do You See?* with sentence frames for parents and children to complete together. Have them paste a folded piece of paper on the bottom of the page to flip up and reveal the animal picture. Children can bring their sheets to school for classmates to guess the identity of their creatures.

Materials
✓ *What Do You See?* sheets
✓ art supplies

LITERATURE LINKS

Go Away, Big Green Monster! by Ed Emberly

Goodness Gracious! by Phil Cummings

I Spy: An Alphabet in Art by Lucy Micklethwait

I Went Walking by Sue Williams

The Monster Book of ABC Sounds by Alan Snow

The Night of the Paper Bag Monster by Helen Craig

One Hungry Monster: A Counting Book in Rhyme by Susan H. O'Keefe

Something Big Has Been Here by Jack Prelutsky

There's Something in My Attic by Mercer Mayer

Visual Magic by David Thornton

What Else Could It Be? by Mario Gomboli

Where the Wild Things Are by Maurice Sendak

WHERE'S YOUR TOOTH?

Everybody helps a young
boy find his lost tooth.

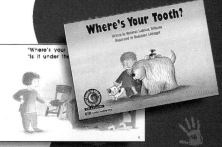

WHERE'S YOUR TOOTH?
Tooth-shaped class book

A bright idea and project from Caroline
Ellis and her kindergartners, Biella School,
Santa Rosa, California

Brainstorm ideas to finish the sentence frame: " 'Where's your
tooth?' asked the ____." Write each child's chosen noun on a
card to help complete the sentence frame on his or her tooth-
shaped page. After children illustrate their sentences, assemble
pages to form a tooth-shaped class book. Encourage children to
add a surprise ending on the last page.

Materials
✓ tooth-shaped
  pages for class
  book
✓ index cards
✓ construction
  paper
✓ art supplies

FAIRY TALE ENDINGS
Tooth-shaped mini-books

A bright idea and project from Caroline Ellis
and her kindergartners, Biella School, Santa
Rosa, California

Assemble books with sentence frames on each page:
" 'Where's your tooth (child's name)? Is it ____? No, no,
no! It's not ____.' " Ask parent volunteers to help children
complete frames with their ideas. On the last page have
children make and attach a pop-up boy or girl tooth fairy
with glittery fabric wings.

Materials
✓ student booklets
  with sentence
  frames
✓ construction paper
✓ glittery fabric for
  fairy wings
✓ art supplies

WRITING FRAMES

"Where's your tooth?"
asked ____.

"Is it under the ____?"

I looked ____.

RELATED SKILLS

• contractions: *here's,
  where's*

• correct usage: *questions*

• parts of speech:
  prepositions

• picture details

• punctuation:
  *quotation marks,
  question marks*

• thought bubbles

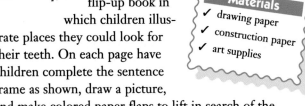

WHERE'S MY TOOTH?
Flip-up books

Make a class flip-up book in which children illustrate places they could look for their teeth. On each page have children complete the sentence frame as shown, draw a picture, and make colored paper flaps to lift in search of the tooth. On the last page they can find their tooth and write, "Here it is!"

Materials
- ✓ drawing paper
- ✓ construction paper
- ✓ art supplies

TOOTH JOURNAL
Journal entries

Make a tooth-shaped journal of blank pages called *Tall Tooth Tales*. As children lose teeth during the school year, have them write tooth stories in the journal with the date and an illustration.

Materials
- ✓ tooth-shaped class book with blank pages
- ✓ art supplies

WHERE DOES THE TOOTH FAIRY LIVE?
Wall story mural

Use *The Tooth Fairy* as an introduction to dental health lessons on brushing and flossing. Have children use the illustrated frame to write and illustrate a wall story mural entitled *Where Does the Tooth Fairy Live?*

Materials
- ✓ *The Tooth Fairy* by Sharon Peters
- ✓ butcher paper
- ✓ art supplies

LEARNING A SKILL

Thought bubbles

Explain that "thought bubbles" in the story show what the cat and dog are thinking. Choose an object in the classroom and brainstorm ideas about what the object might be thinking. Write these words on construction paper thought bubbles and tape them to the object. Show photographs of children taken during the school day and have them tell what they were thinking at the time. Write the words on thought bubbles and paste pictures and bubbles on construction paper around the room for children to read.

Materials
- ✓ construction paper
- ✓ art supplies
- ✓ camera

LINKING SCHOOL TO HOME

Traveling bag

Make a simple "Lost Tooth" traveling bag to send home when children lose a tooth. In the bag include *Where's Your Tooth?* and other related titles and the Tooth Journal described on page 40.

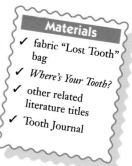

Materials
- ✓ fabric "Lost Tooth" bag
- ✓ *Where's Your Tooth?*
- ✓ other related literature titles
- ✓ Tooth Journal

LITERATURE LINKS

All About Where by Tana Hoban

Hide-and-Seek in the Yellow House by Agatha Rose

Little Rabbit's Loose Tooth by Lucy Bate

Pulling My Leg by Jo Carson

Teeth Week by Nancy Alberts

The Tooth Fairy by Sharon Peters

The Tooth Fairy by Audrey Wood

The Tooth Fairy Book by Deborah Kovacs

Tooth Fairy Magic by Joanne Barkers

The Tooth Tree by Nicholas Heller

Where Is Ben? by Marisabina Russo

Where Is the Bear at School? by Bonnie Larkin Nims

Who Ate It? by Taro Gomi

Who Hid It? by Taro Gomi

WHERE DO MONSTERS LIVE?

Colorful monsters live in homes that match their color and pattern.

WRITING FRAMES

A _____ monster lives in a _____ house.

A _____ child lives in a _____ house.

RELATED SKILLS

- correct usage: *a/an*

- parts of speech: *descriptive words (adjectives), prepositions, verbs*

- picture details: *colors, patterns*

- predicting

- social studies: *shelter*

- vocabulary: *colors, patterns*

ACTIVITY — WHERE DOES A MONSTER LIVE?
Monster house border

In small groups, have children trace around the large monster pattern and use colored construction paper and markers to decorate their creatures. Have them complete the sentence frame: "A _____ monster lives in a _____ house." Paste the sentence strips on the monsters and display creatures along a wall to form a colorful border.

Materials
- ✓ monster pattern (about 12" x 18")
- ✓ construction paper
- ✓ sentence strips
- ✓ art supplies

ACTIVITY — MONSTROUSLY GREAT HOUSES
Wall story

A bright idea and project from Gerianne Smith and her kindergartners, Minnie Gant School, Long Beach, California

Materials
- ✓ construction paper
- ✓ sentence strips
- ✓ art supplies

Have each child cut out a monster house with a door that opens. Invite children to complete the writing frame: "A _____ monster lives in a _____ house," and attach the sentence strips to their houses. Children can decorate their houses and make colorful, matching monsters to place in the doorway.

MONSTER COLLAGE
Patterned monsters

Discuss patterns on wrapping paper and fabric scraps with children. Then have each child glue the materials on a monster shape and write a sentence about his or her creature. Children can also finger paint their monsters, making stripes, polka dots, and mixing colors.

WHERE DO CHILDREN LIVE?
Alternative class book about homes

A bright idea and project from June Swinney and her first graders, New River School, Norwalk, California

Read and discuss *A House Is a House for Me* and *Home*. Provide each child with white construction paper and a blank cardboard paper doll. Invite children to decorate their doll and paste it on the paper. Have them print a descriptive sentence about where they live and draw an illustration. Assemble pages with a colorful cover for class sharing.

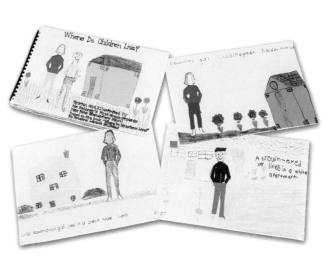

LEARNING A SKILL

Matching patterns and colors

Make copies of blank 2" x 3"
monsters on construction paper
and use markers and stickers to
decorate monster pairs with
identical patterns. Children
can use monsters to play a
concentration game matching monsters with identical patterns.

Materials
- ✓ drawing paper
- ✓ construction paper
- ✓ art supplies

LINKING SCHOOL TO HOME

Designing monsters

Send home construction
paper scraps and ask parents
and children to design a
monster together. They can
use markers, glitter, buttons,
and other materials for deco-
ration. Parents can also help
children write a short story
about their monster.

Materials
- ✓ construction paper scraps
- ✓ art supplies
- ✓ collage materials

Mm is for Monsters!
Your homework is to create a
Marvelous Monster out of the attached
paper. Be creative! Use markers,
glitter, buttons or anything you can
think of to make your monster.
Have fun!

LITERATURE LINKS

A House for Hermit Crab by Eric Carle

A House Is a House for Me by Mary Ann Hoberman

Go Away Big Green Monster by Ed Emberley

Home by Ann Morris

Home in the Sky by Jeannie Baker

Home Place by Crescent Dragonwagon

Mary Wore Her Red Dress, and Henry Wore His Green Sneakers by Merle Peek

The Monster Book of ABC Sounds by Alan Snow

One Hungry Monster: A Counting Book in Rhyme by Susan Heyboer O'Keefe

There's Something in My Attic by Mercer Mayer

The Very Worst Monster by Pat Hutchins

What Color? by Debbie MacKinnon

ALL THROUGH THE WEEK WITH CAT AND DOG

Each morning Dog cooks something and every afternoon Cat eats it!

On Friday morning, Dog made popcorn.

On Friday afternoon, Cat ate the popcorn.

A _ctivity_ THE SECOND WEEK WITH CAT AND DOG
Innovation of original story

A bright idea and project from Darielle Tom and her multi-age primary students, Lee School, Los Alamitos, California

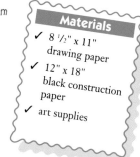

Materials
- ✓ 8 ½" x 11" drawing paper
- ✓ 12" x 18" black construction paper
- ✓ art supplies

Brainstorm ideas for opposite ways Cat and Dog might spend their second week together. For example: "On Monday morning, Cat did push-ups. On Monday afternoon, Dog ate ice cream." By the end of the week, Cat might feel healthy and Dog might feel so bad that they both exercise together. Write each sentence on 8 ½" x 11" paper and have children use crayons or markers to illustrate each page. Paste finished pictures on black construction paper and ask children to sequence the pages. Compile pages to make a class big book with a colorful cover.

A GRAPH IT!
Class graph

Write each day of the week on the chalkboard or chart paper. Beside each day write the food Dog prepared. Have each child choose a favorite among those listed and draw a picture of it. Invite children to glue their pictures on the grid. Ask questions such as: *Which food is most/least popular? How many more/less like cookies than pizzas?*

Materials
- ✓ chart paper
- ✓ drawing paper
- ✓ art supplies

Day	Food	How Many?
Monday	Cookies	
Tuesday	Sandwiches	
Wednesday	pies	

A HOW MANY PIECES?
Fractions (1/4, 1/2, 1 whole)

Invite children to draw their favorite pizza on both paper plates. Have them fold one paper plate pizza in half and cut it on the fold. Ask children to fold the two new pieces in half and cut on the folds. Ask questions to help them compare the four pieces with the whole paper plate pizza. For example: *How many pieces make a whole pizza? How many pieces make half a pizza? If you have three pieces, how many more do you need to make a whole pizza?* Use the pizza pieces to make mini-books about the story characters.

Materials
- ✓ paper plates (two per child)
- ✓ construction paper
- ✓ art supplies

LEARNING A SKILL

Opposites

Point out that whatever Dog made, Cat ate. Invite two children to the front of the class and ask one to stand and the other to do the opposite (sit). Invite another pair to the front and ask one to yell and the other to do the opposite (whisper). Ask children to divide into pairs and take turns performing opposite actions. Take photographs of children for a class book of opposites.

Materials
- ✓ camera
- ✓ construction paper
- ✓ art supplies

LINKING SCHOOL TO HOME

Family activity books

Send home a blank book with a sentence frame on each page:

"On Monday we _____. On Tuesday we _____ . . ." Have children complete the sentence for each day and draw an illustration. Encourage parents to do at least one activity as a family during the week for the book.

Materials
- ✓ blank books with sentence frames
- ✓ art supplies

LITERATURE LINKS

Alexander's Midnight Snack: A Little Elephant's ABC by Catherine Stock

Benny Bakes a Cake by Eve Rice

Blue Hat, Green Hat by Sandra Boynton

Boss for a Week by Libby Handy

Cookie's Week by Cindy Ward

The Cousins by Judith Caseley

Exactly the Opposite by Tana Hoban

I Am the Dog, I Am the Cat by Donald Hall

The Kitten Twins: A Book about Opposites by Marcia Leonard

Opposites by Sandra Boynton

Opposites by Lynn Kightley

BEARS, BEARS, EVERYWHERE

Bears are seen in chairs, in
pairs, and climbing stairs.
Bears are everywhere!

WRITING FRAMES

Bears, bears, everywhere.

Bears in _____.

RELATED SKILLS

• parts of speech: *verbs, nouns, prepositions*

• phonics: *initial consonant b, rhyming words (bear, stair, square)*

• punctuation: *commas*

A*ctivity* FUN WITH BEARS
Stand-up interactive bear book

A bright idea and project from Mary Kurth
and her kindergartners, Black Earth School,
Black Earth, Wisconsin

Write the sentences from *Bears, Bears, Everywhere* on
construction paper strips and paste each sentence on a
sheet of white construction paper. Have children create
the following interactive illustrations for each sentence
in the book:

Make four matching 7" brown paper bears. Paste pairs
of bears together and cover them with clear self-
adhesive paper. Insert a popsicle stick inside the bears
and stand the popsicle stick bears in clay balls.

Other interactive ideas include: a Ferris wheel made
from brass fasteners and colored paper; cotton ball
"cotton candy"; paper pears attached to trees with
yarn; hares on popsicle sticks; paper coins; folded
paper stairs and chairs; pipe cleaner squares attached to the page with yarn;
clear self-adhesive paper covered "ghosts"; spiral pasta "curls" glued on stiff paper
and attached to bears with Velcro strips or paper clips.

Paste paper pockets or plastic bags on each page for storing items and join the
pages accordion-style. Stand the book in a reading corner for children to use.

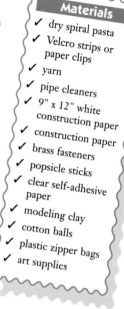

Materials
✓ dry spiral pasta
✓ Velcro strips or
  paper clips
✓ yarn
✓ pipe cleaners
✓ 9" x 12" white
  construction paper
✓ construction paper
✓ brass fasteners
✓ popsicle sticks
✓ clear self-adhesive
  paper
✓ modeling clay
✓ cotton balls
✓ plastic zipper bags
✓ art supplies

BEAR WEAR
Paper bears and clothes

Have children use patterns to make construction paper bears and wrapping paper clothing. Use the tabs (or Velcro) to keep clothes on the bears. Have children put paper bears in different places and say the rhyme, *Bears, bears, everywhere. Bears in ____.* Children can also say, *Bears, bears, everywhere. Bears, bears, what do they wear? This bear wears a ____ and ____.* Make sentence strips for children to match with the bears and their clothing.

This bear wears a T-shirt with blue stripes.

HOME AGAIN BEAR
Class bear and journal

Adopt a teddy bear as a class pet. Give it a name and place it in a take-home bag. Include a small suitcase for the bear with a toothbrush, baby clothing, *Bears, Bears, Everywhere,* one or two other bear books, and a journal in which children can write about and illustrate what they did with the bear.

LEARNING A SKILL

Counting and number sentences

Have children use bear counters, stickers, or stamps to create number sentences such as: "Two red bears went to visit a yellow bear, then there were three."

Four bears went for a walk. One sat down to rest, then there were three.

LINKING SCHOOL TO HOME

Family book

Provide each child with a copy of the text for *Bears, Bears, Everywhere*. Have parents and children use one of the child's teddy bears or other stuffed animals to illustrate scenes in the text. If possible, have them photograph the toy in these scenes, such as in pairs, in squares, and in chairs. Families can use text and photographs to create a book about the stuffed animal in their home.

Bears, bears, everywhere. My bear's in bed.

LITERATURE LINKS

Bear by John Schoenherr

Bear Goes to Town by Anthony Browne

Bear Shadow by Frank Asch

Bears by Ruth Kraus

Bear's Bargain by Frank Asch

Bears in Pairs by Niki Yektai

Berlioz the Bear by Jan Brett

Hi Bears, Bye Bears by Niki Yektai

Jamberry by Bruce Degen

Jessie Bear, What Will You Wear? by Nancy White Carlstrom

One Bear in the Hospital by Caroline Bucknall

Red Bear by Bodel Rikys

CAT AND DOG

Cat and Dog paint similar pictures and appreciate each other's different styles.

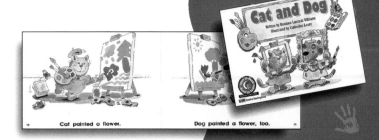

Cat painted a flower. Dog painted a flower, too.

WE CAN DRAW!
Giant pop-up book

A bright idea and project from Jill Tracy and her kindergartners, Helen Lehman School, Santa Rosa, California

Materials

✓ 12" x 18" construction paper
✓ class photo
✓ art supplies

Discuss differences between the drawings made by Cat and Dog and ideas for pictures children could draw with a friend. For example: "Shane draws a great house. Joel can draw a great house, too." Have children work with partners to draw pictures and cut them out for the following class pop-up book:

1. Fold colored construction paper in half lengthwise.

2. Make 3" cuts 3 inches from each end of the paper to form two pop-up folds.

3. On each of the pop-up folds, glue a picture drawn by one pair of children.

4. Paste sentences about the children's work beneath each picture.

5. Glue completed sheets of construction paper together to form a class pop-up book.

Add a pop-up class photo on the last page with the words "We all liked each other's pictures!"

WRITING FRAMES

Cat took out the ____.
Dog took out the ____, too.

Cat painted a ____.
Dog painted a ____, too.

RELATED SKILLS

• correct usage: *too*

• parts of speech: *nouns*

• phonics: *ai (paint)*

• punctuation: *commas, exclamation points, quotation marks*

• suffix: *-ed*

CAN YOU GUESS?
Innovations

Have children write and illustrate their own innovations, using the names of animals and children in the story frame. Read the innovations aloud and have children guess what will happen.

Materials
✓ writing paper
✓ art supplies

FAMOUS CATS AND DOGS
Cartoon book

Have children collect cartoon strips of other famous dog and cat partners such as Garfield and Odie or Mutts. Paste cartoons into a blank book for free time reading fun.

Materials
✓ newspapers
✓ magazines
✓ blank book
✓ art supplies

YOU AND ME
Cooperative partner pictures

Invite children to paint with a friend and take turns being leader and follower. The leader decides what picture to paint and the follower paints the same picture. Discuss which role children preferred and why.

Materials
✓ drawing paper
✓ tempera or watercolor paint
✓ art supplies

LEARNING A SKILL

Correct usage: too

Children can write a new story for Cat and Dog with Dog remaining the "copy cat." In pairs, have children write a new line such as: "Cat took a nap. Dog took a nap, too." To illustrate the page, one partner draws and colors Cat and the other does the same for Dog. Both illustrate the background. Combine all pages in a class book.

Materials
✓ drawing paper
✓ art supplies

LINKING SCHOOL TO HOME

Surprise pictures

Have children work with a family member to make surprise pictures. Each secretly chooses an animal to draw, such as a lion or an elephant. After drawing part of their animal, have them look at the other's pictures. Each person writes the name of the animal they think the other is drawing. They then draw another part of their animal and guess each other's pictures again. Follow this pattern until pictures are complete. Ask how many guesses each person made until correctly guessing each other's animals.

Materials
✓ drawing paper
✓ art supplies

LITERATURE LINKS

Best Friends Together Again by Aliki

Cat on the Mat by Brian Wildsmith

Clifford the Big Red Dog by Norman Bridwell

Friends by Helme Heine

Give a Dog a Bone: Stories, Poems, Jokes, and Riddles about Dogs by Brian Wildsmith

Go, Dog, Go by Philip Eastman

Jake and Rosie by Patricia Lillie

Little Mouse's Painting by Diane Wolkstein

My Dog by Heidi Goennel

New Friends, True Friends, Stuck-Like-Glue Friends by Virginia Kroll

So Many Cats! by Beatrice Schenk De Regniers

We Are Best Friends by Aliki

CINDERELLA DRESSED IN YELLOW

This is a colorful adaptation of the familiar Cinderella jump-rope rhyme.

WRITING FRAMES

Cinderella dressed in _____ went downstairs to/and _____ _____ _____.

How many _____ did she _____?

RELATED SKILLS

• correct usage: *questions*

• numbers: *counting, one-to-one correspondence*

• phonics: *rhyming words (red/head; blue/shoe; green/cream)*

• punctuation: *question marks*

• rhythm

• vocabulary: *colors*

A*ctivity* CINDERELLA UPDATE
"Buddy" rewrites

A bright idea and project from Cori Giacchino, her kindergartners, and their fourth grade "buddies," Los Alamitos School, Los Alamitos, California

Materials
✓ 12" x 18" white paper
✓ watercolor or tempera paint
✓ art supplies

Assign an older "buddy" from another class to work with each child. Have children brainstorm innovations to the story using sentence frames from the book. Provide each pair of children with a sheet of 12" x 18" paper and have them fold it in three horizontal sections. In each third have one partner print the new verse. The other partner illustrates and paints pictures to go with each verse. Assemble each rewrite into a class big book with a decorated, laminated cover.

CLASS RHYMES
Class innovation big book

Have children choose other favorite story characters or their own names and use the *Cinderella* rhyme pattern to create new verses for a class big book. Invite each child to illustrate the verse on his or her page.

Materials
- ✓ drawing paper
- ✓ construction paper
- ✓ art supplies

The big bad wolf dressed in a top hat, went out the door and chased a fat rat.

Clifford, Clifford dressed in red. Fell asleep and broke the bed.

COUNTING WITH CINDERELLA
Counting book

Have children work as a group to write the text for a *Cinderella* counting book.

Copy the text on a page for each child to cut apart. Have children glue sentences to the bottom of each page in a prestapled book and make illustrations. Children can use the kiss stamp to make kisses, white glue to make clear-drying "bumps," shoes cut from magazines, and construction paper ice cream scoops.

Materials
- ✓ prestapled books
- ✓ copies of new text
- ✓ "kiss" stamp
- ✓ stamp pad
- ✓ magazines
- ✓ construction paper
- ✓ art supplies

Cinderella has one shoe.

Cinderella has four kisses.

Cinderella has three scoops.

CINDERELLA ROUND
Rhyme game

Seat children in a circle to play Cinderella Round. Each child repeats a line from the rhyme until someone says, *How many kisses did he get?* The next child says a number from one to ten and each player counts off that number in sequence. The child next to the last counting person starts the next verse. Encourage children to make innovations and add rhythm by clapping or drumming.

Materials
- ✓ *Cinderella* rhyme
- ✓ drum

A C T I V I T Y

CINDERELLAS AND CINDERFELLAS
Paper dolls

Have children use the person pattern to make tagboard dolls and the clothing patterns to make colored clothes. They can "dress" their dolls to retell the story and dramatize new versions of the rhyme. Keep the paper clothes in place by using tabs or Velcro. Print new verses about the dolls on construction paper to display as a bulletin board story with Cinderellas and Cinderfellas.

Materials
- ✓ person patterns
- ✓ clothing patterns with tabs (dress, T-shirt, shorts, skirt, trousers)
- ✓ tagboard
- ✓ construction paper
- ✓ art supplies

LEARNING A SKILL
Problem solving

Provide children with dried beans and cereal "O's" to use as counters to answer the questions in *Cinderella*. Ask comparison questions such as: *Did Cinderella get more bumps on her head or more home runs? How many more home runs did she get?* Children can use counters to discover the answers.

Materials
- ✓ dried beans
- ✓ cereal "O's"

LINKING SCHOOL TO HOME
Jump-rope rhyme

Reread the story several times so children know the *Cinderella* rhyme by heart. Ask family members to hold a rope for children to jump as they recite the chant. As a variation, have children count off their jumps after each verse until they miss or get tired.

Materials
- ✓ jump ropes

LITERATURE LINKS

Anna Banana: 101 Jump-Rope Rhymes by Joanna Cole

Cinder-Elly by Frances Minters

Color by Christina Rosetti

Color Dance by Ann Jonas

Colors by Pascale de Bourgoing

Colors Everywhere by Tana Hoban

The Green Queen by Nick Sharratt

Numbears: A Counting Book by Kathleen Hague

Paintbox Penguins: A Book about Colors by Marcia Leonard

The Paper Bag Princess by Robert Munsch

Play Rhymes by Marc Brown

Purple, Green, and Yellow by Robert Munsch

CITY MOUSE AND COUNTRY MOUSE

A city mouse and country mouse trade places.

City Mouse eats cheese.　Country Mouse eats seeds.

A CITY LIFE VS. COUNTRY LIFE
Comparison lists and murals

A bright idea and project from Bea Tamo and her special day summer school class, Hopkinson School, Los Alamitos, California

Brainstorm the benefits of living in the city or in the country. For example: "The city is a good place to visit a museum" and "The country is a great place to ride a horse." Assign half the class to work on a "city" mural and the others to work on a "country" mural. Each group can illustrate their ideas and label their artwork with sentences.

Materials
- ✓ butcher paper
- ✓ tempera paint
- ✓ sentence strips
- ✓ art supplies
- ✓ collage materials

WRITING FRAMES

City Mouse eats ____.
Country Mouse eats ____.

City Mouse sleeps in a ____. Country Mouse sleeps in a ____. . .

RELATED SKILLS

- contractions: *didn't, let's*
- drawing conclusions
- parts of speech: *verbs*
- phonics: *hard c (country), soft c (city), ee (sleep), ea (eats)*
- picture clues
- punctuation: *quotation marks*
- sequencing
- vocabulary: *opposites*

City　　　　　Country

The city is a good place to visit a museum.

The country is a great place to ride a horse.

MOUSE OPPOSITES
Paper plate mice

Provide each child with two paper plates and construction paper. Have children decorate one paper plate as City Mouse and the other as Country Mouse. Children then paste the paper plates together and add a tongue depressor "handle." Invite children to use their mice to retell the story.

Materials
✓ paper plates
✓ construction paper
✓ tongue depressors
✓ art supplies

HOME SWEET HOME
Habitat dioramas

Have children work with partners to create a shoe box diorama showing different mice habitats such as the forest or desert. They can make mice from rocks by adding wiggly eyes and felt ears and tails. Children can make scenery and labels from colored construction paper for their dioramas and explain the habitats to classmates.

Materials
✓ shoe boxes
✓ rocks
✓ wiggly eyes
✓ felt (gray, white, brown, pink, black)
✓ construction paper
✓ art supplies

MOUSE BITES
Mouse cookies

Make mouse bites as follows:

1. Place the cookie dough in the freezer for about one hour.

2. Slice the dough into ¼"-thick, round slices.

3. Cut ¼ of the slices into fourths to form ears.

4. Place two "ears" on each round slice on a cookie sheet.

5. Use the M&Ms for eyes and a chocolate chip for a nose.

6. Bake at 350°F for 12 minutes or until golden brown.

Read *If You Give a Mouse a Cookie* as children eat their mouse bites.

Materials
✓ refrigerator cookie dough
✓ chocolate chips
✓ M&Ms
✓ cookie sheets
✓ oven
✓ knife (adult use only)
✓ *If You Give Mouse a Cookie* by Laura J. Numeroff

CITY MOUSE AND COUNTRY MOUSE
Class big book

A bright idea and project from Carol Gauntlett and her first graders, Lincoln School, Long Beach, California

Paste a copy of each sentence from the story on white paper for children to illustrate. Laminate the new pages and challenge students to place them in sequence. Combine pages to make a class big book for sharing.

Materials
- ✓ copies of sentences from *City Mouse and Country Mouse*
- ✓ white construction paper
- ✓ art supplies

LEARNING A SKILL
Quotation marks

Have children cut apart a favorite cartoon strip and paste each box on construction paper. Use quotation marks to rewrite each box.

Materials
- ✓ cartoon strips
- ✓ construction paper
- ✓ art supplies

LINKING SCHOOL TO HOME
Fable puppets and pictures

City Mouse and Country Mouse is a fable. Ask parents and children to research other fables such as those by Aesop or Gerald McDermott. They can read the stories together and choose a favorite to learn. Children can retell their fables to classmates using stick puppets or pictures.

Materials
- ✓ fables
- ✓ construction paper
- ✓ popsicle sticks
- ✓ art supplies

LITERATURE LINKS

A Visit to the Country by Herschel Johnson

A Year in the Country by Douglas Florian

City Cat, Country Cat by Patricia Cleveland-Peck

City Mouse and Country Mouse by John Wallner

City Sounds by Rebecca Emberley

If You Give a Mouse a Cookie by Laura J. Numeroff

Town and Country by Alice and Martin Provensen

The Trouble with the Johnsons by Mark Teague

Two Tiny Mice by Alan Baker

Wake Up, City! by Alvin Tresselt

Wake Up, Farm! by Alvin Tresselt

Window by Jeannie Baker

DOWN ON THE FARM

This song explores the sounds made by farm animals and is available on Greg and Steve's *Playin' Favorites* (Youngheart Music).

WRITING FRAMES

The _____ on the _____
says, "_____, _____, _____!"

The _____ on the _____
says, "_____!" down on
the _____.

RELATED SKILLS

• sounds

• punctuation: *commas, quotation marks*

• phonics: *oo (doodle), oi (oink), ee (hee), short o*

• parts of speech: *nouns, prepositions*

*A*ctivity

THE THREE LITTLE PIGS
Class storybook and map

Bright ideas and projects from Miss Luedeker, Mrs. Lynes, and their first and second graders, Olde Orchard Alternative School, Columbus, Ohio

Materials
✓ large sheets of brown paper
✓ construction paper
✓ drawing paper
✓ loose leaf rings
✓ art supplies
✓ camera

1. Create a story innovation using the rhyme patterns in *Down on the Farm* and a traditional tale such as *The Three Little Pigs*. Write each verse on a separate sheet of construction paper for children to illustrate. Laminate and compile pages for a class book. The first (or last) page can feature a class photograph surrounded by children's signatures.

2. Join large sheets of brown paper to form a 6' square. Have small groups illustrate each new verse on drawing paper and paste pictures and verses on the brown paper square. Children can add speech bubbles to their pictures and make arrows to connect events on the story map. Photograph children as they work, and display pictures in the middle of the brown paper.

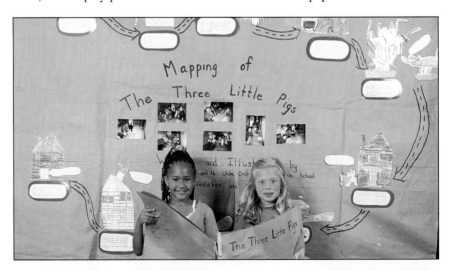

BARNYARD CHATTER
Three-dimensional animal puppets

Have each child draw and color a favorite animal from the story on 12" x 18" white paper. Trace and cut out a second copy of the animal and staple the edges of the two shapes together leaving the top open. Color the back of the animal, stuff the insides with crumpled newspaper, and staple the animal closed. Have children use creatures as puppets or as a bulletin board display with speech bubbles showing the words spoken by each animal.

Materials
- ✓ 12" x 18" white paper
- ✓ drawing paper
- ✓ newspaper
- ✓ art supplies

DEEP IN THE JUNGLE
Class song

Make a list of jungle animals and their sounds on the chalkboard. Have each child draw a jungle animal and use the sentence patterns in *Down on the Farm* to create verses for a song entitled *Deep in the Jungle*. Compile illustrations and verses in a book and sing the new class song. Children can also help write and illustrate verses for songs about ocean, desert, and polar habitats.

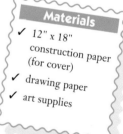

Materials
- ✓ 12" x 18" construction paper (for cover)
- ✓ drawing paper
- ✓ art supplies

The monkey in the tree says, "Chee, chee, chee. Chee, chee, chee. Chee, chee, chee."

LEARNING A SKILL

Using "said" with quotation marks

Children can decorate socks or make stick puppets to create animal characters. Help children write the words their puppet speaks using *said* and quotation marks. Older children can practice using a comma followed by quotation marks.

Materials
✓ old clean socks
✓ rubber bands
✓ popsicle sticks
✓ construction paper
✓ collage materials
✓ art supplies

LINKING SCHOOL TO HOME

Song

Parents and children can create a parody of *Down on the Farm* entitled *All Through My House*. They can explore the sounds within their home and write their own verses using the rhyme patterns in the original song. Families may illustrate their stories/songs with photographs for others to enjoy.

Materials
✓ writing paper
✓ art supplies

LITERATURE LINKS

A Visit to the Farm by Coby Hol

Buzz, Buzz, Buzz by Byron Barton

Color Farm by Lois Ehlert

Farm Noises by Jane Miller

Hoot, Howl, Hiss by Michelle Koch

Moo, Moo, Brown Cow by Jakki Wood

My Barn by Craig Brown

My Farm by Alison Lester

Noisy Neighbors: A Book about Animal Sounds by Marcia Leonard

Oh, What a Noisy Farm by Harriet Ziefert

Roar and More by Karla Kuskin

Who Took the Farmer's Hat? by Joan Nodset

THE GIRAFFE MADE HER LAUGH

A cumulative story shows the funny antics of a giraffe who makes a queen laugh.

The cat just sat.   But the giraffe made her laugh.

THE LION KEPT HIM CRYIN'
Class cumulative book

A bright idea and project from Gina Lems-Tardif and her first graders, Lee Elementary School, Los Alamitos, California

Brainstorm ideas to make a class cumulative book using the rhyme patterns in *The Giraffe Made Her Laugh*. Fold each length of white paper in half to form pages for the class book. Help children wash each page in blue watercolor paint, leaving the bottom 2" strip white for sentences. Write children's verses on each page and have them make illustrations using construction paper and collage materials. Outline pages with black marker. Have children draw themselves and print their names on white paper squares to paste on the last page with the heading "Written and illustrated by . . . . "

Materials
- ✓ 17" x 46" lengths of white paper
- ✓ construction paper
- ✓ blue watercolor paint
- ✓ black markers
- ✓ wrapping paper
- ✓ aluminum foil
- ✓ 3" squares of white paper
- ✓ art supplies
- ✓ collage materials

WRITING FRAMES

The _____. (A)

But the _____! (B)

The _____. (C)

The _____. (A)

But the _____! (B)

RELATED SKILLS

- cumulative sentences
- phonics: *rhyming words (giraffe/laugh; cat/sat; sheep/sleep)*
- sequencing

The Lion Kept Him Cryin'

The dog played pog.

The bear dyed her hair.

The pig was big.

The monkey looked punky.

But the lion kept him cryin'.

THE NAPPING HOUSE
Finger puppet retellings

Read other cumulative stories such as *The Napping House* and *Shoes from Grandpa*. Help children decorate strips of paper to make finger puppets to represent characters from one of the stories. They can wear these finger puppets as they retell the story for classmates.

Materials

✓ *The Napping House* by Audrey Wood
✓ *Shoes from Grandpa* by Mem Fox
✓ 1" x 2" paper strips
✓ construction paper
✓ art supplies

TELL IT AGAIN
Sequencing

Write the story text on sentence strips and have children make illustrations for each sentence. Children can sequence the text and pictures in a pocket chart. Hint: Make one set of the following sentences for repeated use.

The snake baked a cake.

The cow took a bow.

The sheep went to sleep.

The cat just sat.

But the giraffe made me laugh!

Materials

✓ sentence strips
✓ construction paper
✓ pocket chart
✓ art supplies

KEEP HER LAUGHIN'
Flannel board story retelling

A **C** **T** **I** **V** **I** **T** **Y**

Have children work in small groups to draw and cut out pictures of each story character. They can attach strips of sandpaper or Velcro to the back of each picture and use their characters to retell the story on a flannel board for another class.

Materials
- ✓ drawing paper
- ✓ sandpaper or Velcro strips
- ✓ flannel board
- ✓ art supplies

LEARNING A SKILL

Phonics: rhyming words

Have children find rhyming words in the story and list them in columns on the chalkboard. Children can go on a word hunt around the classroom to find more rhyming words for each column. Use the list of rhyming words to write class innovations to the story.

Materials
- ✓ drawing paper
- ✓ art supplies

LINKING SCHOOL TO HOME

Sack story innovations

Children can create a cumulative sack story innovation to share with their family. Have them decorate a paper bag with a construction paper picture of themselves. Children can also draw and cut out pictures of animals for their own version of the story such as *The bear sat in a chair.* Have them retell their story to parents as they pull story pieces from their bag.

Materials
- ✓ small brown paper bags
- ✓ construction paper
- ✓ art supplies

LITERATURE LINKS

The Cat Came Back retold by Bill Slavin

I Know an Old Lady Who Swallowed a Fly illustrated by Glen Rounds

If You Give a Mouse a Cookie by Laura J. Numeroff

In a Cabin in a Wood adapted by Darcie McNally

The Jacket I Wear in the Snow by Shirley Neitzel

Moose in the Garden by Nancy White Carlstrom

The Napping House by Audrey Wood

One Monday Morning by Uri Shulevitz

Over the Steamy Swamp by Paul Geraghty

Shoes from Grandpa by Mem Fox

Sitting on the Farm by Bob King

What's for Lunch? by John Schindel

MR. NOISY

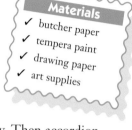

Mr. Noisy makes a lot of noise but everyone misses his noise when he is quiet.

WRITING FRAMES

Mr. Noisy made noise when he _____.

Mr. Noisy _____ quietly.

A _____ makes a _____ noise.

RELATED SKILLS

• contractions: *it's, where's*

• correct usage: *too*

• parts of speech: *proper nouns, verbs*

• phonics: *oi (noise)*

• punctuation: *exclamation points, periods, abbreviations, quotation marks*

• suffixes: *-ed, -ly*

• vocabulary: *sound words (onomatopoeia)*

*A*ctivity

ENERGY CAT
Hanging wall story

A bright idea and project from Candice Siu and her first graders, Lee School, Los Alamitos, California

Materials
✓ butcher paper
✓ tempera paint
✓ drawing paper
✓ art supplies

Use the language pattern in *Mr. Noisy* to create class books about other topics. For example, make a book focusing on energy featuring a new character, Energy Cat. First fold a long length of butcher paper in half horizontally. Then accordion-fold the length of paper and cut the shape of a cat's head paper-doll style. Have children paint pictures of how Energy Cat exerts energy and outline their pictures with black marker. Help children use the *Mr. Noisy* sentence patterns to write or dictate sentences about their pictures. On each cat-shaped page, paste a child's picture and sentence. Display the wall story for class sharing.

IT'S A NOISY WORLD
Wall story and book

A bright idea and project from Candice Siu and her first graders, Lee School, Los Alamitos, California

Have children sponge paint the earth and sky on butcher paper and paint characters and objects from the story on drawing paper. Cut out and paste pictures on the scene. Help children write the sounds made by their pictures on colored paper speech bubbles to paste near the illustrations.

Materials
- ✓ butcher paper
- ✓ tempera paint
- ✓ sponges
- ✓ drawing paper
- ✓ colored paper
- ✓ art supplies

LISTEN IN
Sound lists

Give each child a sheet of paper folded in half vertically. Set the timer for five minutes and have children listen to the noises around them. Ask them to write noisy sounds on one side and quiet sounds on the other. After five minutes compare lists to find whether children listed more noisy or quiet sounds. As an alternative, prepare a tape of noises and have children identify the sounds by drawing a picture or writing the words.

Materials
- ✓ drawing paper
- ✓ timer
- ✓ cassette tape of recorded sounds
- ✓ cassette player
- ✓ art supplies

LEARNING A SKILL

-ed words

Have children locate and make a list of all the *-ed* words in *Mr. Noisy*. Explain that *-ed* is an ending, and ask children to underline the root words. Challenge them to search other books for words ending with *-ed* and add these to the list. Older children can sort *-ed* words into two lists of words ending with *d* or *t* sounds.

Materials
✓ *Learn to Read* books
✓ writing paper

LINKING SCHOOL TO HOME

Accordion books

Help children make a four-page, accordion-style book entitled *When Do You Make Noise?* At the top of each page, print: "I make noise when I ____. But I ____ quietly." Parents can help children complete the first page about themselves and the other pages about different family members. Have children illustrate each page with a picture of the person making the noise or being quiet, and share their books with classmates.

Materials
✓ drawing paper
✓ art supplies

LITERATURE LINKS

The Banging Book by Bill Grossman

The Country Noisy Book by Margaret Wise Brown

Let's Make a Noise by Amy MacDonald

Mr. Mumble by Peter Catalanotto

The Noisemaker by Judith Caseley

Noisy Nora by Rosemary Wells

Quiet by Peter Parnall

The Quiet Mother and the Noisy Little Boy by Charlotte Zolotow

Shhhh by Kevin Henkes

This Quiet Lady by Charlotte Zolotow

Ty's One-Man Band by Mildred Walter

The Very Quiet Cricket by Eric Carle

SCAREDY CAT

Animals chase each other but discover they can all be friends.

Scaredy Cat chased the mouse.   The mouse chased Scaredy Cat.

DON'T BE SCARED OF ME!

Stand-up animal puppets

A bright idea and project from Mary Kurth and her kindergartners, Black Earth School, Black Earth, Wisconsin.

Have each child draw an animal on tagboard, print its name underneath, and make a matching word card. Help children glue their pictures to milk cartons to make stand-up puppets. Children then sit in a circle and recite a line from the story such as, *Scaredy Cat chased the mouse.* The child with the mouse puppet places it in the center and responds, *The mouse chased Scaredy Cat.* Continue until all animals are in the circle. Students remove their puppets by reciting, *"Don't be scared of me!" said the _____.* Place puppets in the circle and have students place their word cards near the animals as they recite the language pattern. Store puppets and word cards in a box or basket for children to use during free time.

Materials

✓ 5" x 8" tagboard
✓ empty 1-pint milk cartons
✓ black markers
✓ wood cards
✓ art supplies

WRITING FRAMES

Scaredy Cat chased the _____.

The _____ chased Scaredy Cat.

"Don't be scared of me!" said the _____.

A _____ chased the _____.

RELATED SKILLS

• conflict resolution

• contractions

• parts of speech: *proper nouns*

• phonics: *sc (scaredy), ch (chased)*

• punctuation: *capital letters, exclamation points, quotation marks*

SCAREDY CAT AND FRIENDS
Paper plate masks

Invite children to draw story character faces on paper plates, adding pipe cleaner whiskers. They can wear the masks to retell the story and create new adventures for Scaredy Cat and his friends.

Materials
- ✓ paper plates
- ✓ pipe cleaners
- ✓ elastic
- ✓ art supplies

CONFLICT RESOLUTION
Conflict resolution role play

Read the story and talk about how Scaredy Cat felt. Explain that sometimes people talk or act inappropriately when they feel uncomfortable or insecure. Wearing animals masks, have children role play what the animals might say to Scaredy Cat instead of chasing him. They can also role play ways to introduce themselves when they meet new people.

Materials
- ✓ animal masks from *Scaredy Cat and Friends* activity

WHAT MAKES ME AFRAID?
Paper doll stories

Provide each child with two construction paper dolls. Have children decorate the front of one doll and staple the two doll shapes together at the top. Inside the doll "book" children can draw or write what makes them afraid. Invite students to share their ideas in small groups.

Materials
- ✓ construction paper dolls
- ✓ art supplies

LEARNING A SKILL

Contractions

Decorate a box with wrapping paper and the title *Contractions*. On strips of construction paper, print words that make contractions, such as *where is* and *I am*. Fold the papers so the words become contractions and add apostrophes in the correct places. Invite children to look for contractions in other stories and add new contractions to the box for children to manipulate and read.

Materials
- ✓ small box
- ✓ wrapping paper
- ✓ construction paper
- ✓ art supplies

LINKING SCHOOL TO HOME

Discussing fears

It is common for children at this stage of development to have normal childhood fears. Children can take home a copy of *Scaredy Cat* to read with family members. Ask parent and child to discuss one of the child's fears and one way to confront that fear. Children can write and illustrate their strategies and bring them to school to share with classmates.

Materials
- ✓ *Scaredy Cat*
- ✓ drawing paper
- ✓ art supplies

LITERATURE LINKS

Best Friends Wear Pink Tutus by Sheri Brownrigg

The Dancing Cat by Justine Rendal

Four Fierce Kittens by Joyce Dunbar

Frog Is Frightened by Max Velthuigs

Go Away, William by Margaret Carter

Have You Seen My Cat? by Eric Carle

I Wouldn't Be Scared by John Sabraw

Leo the Late Bloomer by Robert Kraus

Let's Be Friends by Caroline Ness

Nellie: A Cat on Her Own by Natalie Babbitt

Think Hippo! by Wendy Smith

Will I Have a Friend? by Miriam Cohen

THERE'S A MONSTER IN THE TREE

Monsters are discovered in unusual places in this repetitious, musical rhyme.

WRITING FRAME

There's a _____ in the _____, in the _____.

There's a _____ in the _____,
And she's _____ _____ _____.

RELATED SKILLS

- contractions: *he's, she's, there's*

- parts of speech: *prepositions*

- phonics: *rhyming words (tree/three; door/floor; hall/ball; kitchen/chicken; pot/hot; bed/said; bedroom/red broom)*

- punctuation: *commas, quotation marks*

- suffix: *-ing*

A̶ ̶FLUORESCENT MONSTERS
Monster artwork and verses

A bright idea and project from Marcia Fries and her multi-age students, Lee School, Los Alamitos, California

Invite children to draw a monster on white construction paper and outline it with fluorescent glue. When dry, have them color their monsters with chalk and cut them out. Help children write a verse for their monster on colored construction paper, and add details to decorate a scene for the bulletin board.

Materials
✓ construction paper
✓ fluorescent glue
✓ colored chalk
✓ art supplies

THERE'S A PENGUIN ON THE ICE
Alternative mini-books

A bright idea from Cathy Young and Caroline Ellis, Biella School, Santa Rosa, California

Materials
- ✓ chart paper
- ✓ student copies of class rhymes
- ✓ construction paper
- ✓ art supplies

Brainstorm ideas for places where a favorite animal might be found. For example, a penguin might be in water or on ice. Write these nouns on a chart and add rhyming words to make new verses using the original story's rhyme patterns. Make copies of the new verses for children to illustrate. Staple pages to form individual mini-books with construction paper covers.

THERE'S A MONSTER IN THE . . .
Monster flip-books

Have children fold paper in half so the fold is at the top. This will be the cover. On the cover have children write: "There's a monster in the . . . ." On the inside have them draw a picture of their monster showing where it is and what it is doing. Beneath the picture they can write a word to complete the sentence frame. Display monster flips for children to read or staple six or eight flips together to form books.

Materials
- ✓ drawing paper
- ✓ art supplies

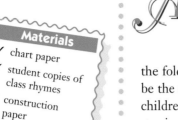

MONSTER BOOKS
Individual monster-shaped books

Have each child create a construction paper monster and staple blank pages on the front to make a book. Children can write their own monster rhymes or stories on these pages to share with classmates.

Materials
- ✓ construction paper
- ✓ drawing paper
- ✓ art supplies

LEARNING A SKILL

Prepositions

Invite each child to draw, cut out, and glue a construction paper monster on a popsicle stick. Ask children to place their monsters *in* something, such as a desk, and model the text by saying where their monster is located. Ask children to place their monsters *on* something and then model the pattern again emphasizing the word *on*. Use this exercise with children to explore other prepositions.

Materials
- ✓ construction paper
- ✓ popsicle sticks
- ✓ art supplies

LINKING SCHOOL TO HOME

Paper bag monsters

Have children make paper bag monsters and decorate them with construction paper. They can take their paper bag puppets home and create monster rhymes to perform with their families.

Materials
- ✓ small brown paper bags
- ✓ construction paper
- ✓ art supplies

LITERATURE LINKS

Go Away Monsters, Lickety Split! by Nancy E. Cooney

Hershel and the Hanukkah Goblins by Eric Kimmel

Looking After Your First Monster by Frank Rodgers

The Lunch Box Monster by Carolyn Dinan

The Monster Bed by Jeanne Willis

The Monster Book of ABC Sounds by Alan Snow

The Monster Storm by Jeanne Willis

One Monster After Another by Mercer Mayer

Silly Billy! by Pat Hutchins

Skateboard Monsters by Daniel Kirk

There's a Monster Under My Bed by James Howe

The Very Worst Monster by Pat Hutchins

WAY DOWN SOUTH

Large animals cry when smaller animals step on their toes in this adaptation of the traditional song.

A WAY UP NORTH
Class book

Materials
✓ drawing paper
✓ art supplies

Examine pictures of animals and plants from the Northern Hemisphere and brainstorm ideas for new verses about them. Use the sentence patterns in *Way Down South* as a guide. For example: "Way up north where birch trees grow, a fly stepped on a wolf's toe . . . ." Write each new verse on drawing paper and have children illustrate their pages for a class book entitled *Way Up North*.

WRITING FRAMES

Way down south where _____ grow, a _____ stepped on a/an _____'s toe.

The _____ said with tears in his eyes, "Pick on somebody your own size!"

Way up north _____ . . .

Way out west _____ . . .

Way back east _____ . . .

RELATED SKILLS

• correct usage: *a/an*

• geography: *location, plants, animals*

• making comparisons

• phonics: *rhyming words (grow/toe; eyes/size)*

• punctuation: *apostrophes, commas, quotation marks, exclamation points*

• vocabulary: *compound words*

GOLDILOCKS AND THE THREE BEARS
Size comparisons

Read *Goldilocks and the Three Bears* and have children make stick puppets for the bears, chairs, beds, and bowls of porridge. Children can use the puppets to compare sizes as they retell the story. Ask parents to share family pictures which show their child's growth since birth. They can send in pictures of their children as newborn babies and in their first, second, third, fourth, and fifth years. Invite children to share their photographs and observations about their own size differences.

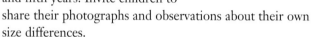

Materials
- ✓ *Goldilocks and the Three Bears* (Traditional)
- ✓ construction paper
- ✓ popsicle sticks
- ✓ art supplies
- ✓ children's photographs

BIG AND SMALL
Story adaptations

Invite each child to draw and color a picture of a big and small animal. Have children outline the animals with black marker and cut them out. Using *Way Down South* sentence frames, have children write verses about their big and small animals. Display pictures and sentences on a bulletin board. Help children make speech bubbles to show what their animals are saying.

Materials
- ✓ drawing paper
- ✓ tempera paint
- ✓ black markers
- ✓ construction paper
- ✓ art supplies

ELEPHANT FEET
Measurements

Look at the elephant's foot on page three of *Way Down South* and ask children what an elephant's footprint might look like. Have students trace elephant footprint patterns on gray paper to make footprints. Children can use their elephant footprints to estimate and measure different items such as the width and length of the classroom. They can also lie on the floor and ask a friend to measure their height in elephant feet. Make a simple sheet for children to record their measurements.

Materials
- ✓ elephant footprint patterns
- ✓ gray construction paper
- ✓ record sheet
- ✓ art supplies

LEARNING A SKILL

Compound words

Decorate a box with wrapping paper and label it *Compound Words*. Write compound words from the story on construction paper strips and cut each word to make puzzle pieces. Provide time for children to make and read compound words with class-mates. Encourage them to look for compound words in other *Learn to Read* books, such as *Rain*, and add these words to the box.

Materials
- ✓ small box
- ✓ wrapping paper
- ✓ construction paper
- ✓ art supplies
- ✓ *Rain*

LINKING SCHOOL TO HOME

Family verses

Have family members use *Way Down South* frames to write and illustrate a verse about a family member or pet. Children can share their verses and pictures with classmates.

Materials
- ✓ copies of *Way Down South* sentence frames
- ✓ drawing paper
- ✓ art supplies

LITERATURE LINKS

Down by the Bay by Raffi

The Farmer in the Dell: A Singing Rhyme illustrated by Mary M. Rae

Goldilocks and the Three Bears (Traditional)

Large as Life by Julia Finzel

Little Big Mouse by Nurit Karlin

Look Again! The Second Ultimate Spot-the-Difference Book by A.J. Wood

Mary Had a Little Lamb by Sarah J. Hale

Old Noah's Elephants adapted by Warren Ludwig

Play Rhymes by Marc Brown

"Stand Back," Said the Elephant, "I'm Going to Sneeze!" by Patricia Thomas

Time for School, Nathan! by Lulu Delacre

Zachary Raffles by Dennis Kyle

WHO WILL HELP?

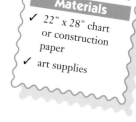

A mouse makes applesauce without any help in this *Little Red Hen* adaptation.

"Who will help me peel the apples?"

Who Will Help?
Adapted by Rosanne Lanczak Williams
Illustrated by Mary Thelen

WRITING FRAMES

"Who will help me _____ the _____?"

"Not me!" said the _____.

"Not me!" said the _____.

"Not me!" said the _____.

_____ did not help _____.

RELATED SKILLS

• phonics: *double consonants (ll, pp)*

• punctuation: *commas, exclamation points, question marks, quotation marks*

• sequencing

• speech bubbles

• writing directions

𝒜CTIVITY

WHO WILL HELP?
Story charts

A bright idea and project from Bev Maeda and her multi-age students, Rolling Hills School, Fullerton, California

Invite children to work with partners to create innovations on *Who Will Help?* Have them fold paper to form two rows of four rectangles. Working from left to right, have children draw a picture in each space to show someone asking for help with a task and being refused. Children can then title their story charts and share their work with classmates.

Materials
✓ 22" x 28" chart or construction paper
✓ art supplies

WHAT DO YOU THINK?
Chart of written reactions and artwork

A bright idea and project from Bev Maeda and her multi-age students, Rolling Hills School, Fullerton, California

Materials
- ✓ butcher paper
- ✓ drawing paper
- ✓ tempera paint
- ✓ art supplies

Discuss whether the mouse should share the applesauce with the other animals. Have each child write reasons for his or her response in a speech bubble, and paint a large mouse (about 8" x 13") on drawing paper. Children then cut out their mice and paste them on the butcher paper with their speech bubbles. Display the response chart where children can read their classmates' work.

BAKED APPLES
Cooperative baking

Have children work in cooperative groups with adult supervision to bake apples as follows:

1. Peel apples halfway and remove the core from the top, just past the seeds.

2. Place apples in a shallow baking dish.

3. Cover the bottom of the baking dish with ¼" water.

4. Place a pat of butter in each core and sprinkle the apples with cinnamon and brown sugar.

5. Microwave apples for about ten minutes.

6. Serve baked apples hot or cold, with cream or vanilla ice cream.

Children can share ideas about why cooperation is helpful and record their thoughts in their journals.

Materials
- ✓ Macintosh apples (one per child)
- ✓ vegetable peelers
- ✓ apple corers or knives (adult use only)
- ✓ shallow baking dishes
- ✓ butter
- ✓ cinnamon
- ✓ brown sugar
- ✓ microwave
- ✓ cream or vanilla ice cream
- ✓ serving bowls
- ✓ plastic spoons

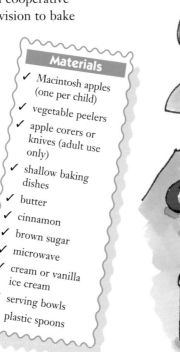

LET'S HELP OUT
Speech bubbles

Have children brainstorm ways they can help others at home or school.

Encourage them to write sentences about their actions and cut around the sentences to form speech bubbles. Children can paint a portrait of themselves on drawing paper and paste on their speech bubbles. Assemble their artwork in a class book.

Materials
- ✓ drawing paper
- ✓ tempera or water-color paint
- ✓ art supplies

LEARNING A SKILL
Sequencing

Write the story on sentence strips and have children make illustrations using cut paper. Children can sequence the text and pictures in a pocket chart. Hint: Make one set of the following sentences for repeated use:

"Not me!" said the duck.

"Not me!" said the rabbit.

"Not me!" said the cow.

Materials
- ✓ sentence strips
- ✓ colored paper
- ✓ pocket chart
- ✓ art supplies

LINKING SCHOOL TO HOME
Coupon books and story rewrites

Staple pages to make mini coupon books for children to decorate with ideas for helping at home. Children can give coupon books to their parents to redeem. Have families rewrite the story so that everyone helps and ends up enjoying themselves.

Materials
- ✓ drawing paper
- ✓ art supplies

LITERATURE LINKS

Apples and Pumpkins by Anne Rockwell

Crossing the Bridge by Emily Arnold McCully

The Fabulous Fireworks Family by James Flora

The Fire Station by Robert Munsch

Helping Is Fun by Alice Greenspan

Johnny Appleseed by Steven Kellogg

Latkes and Applesauce by Fran Manushkin

The Little Red Hen illustrated by Lucinda McQueen

The Minpins by Roald Dahl

Reuben and the Fire by Merle Good

Smoky Night by Eve Bunting

Stone Soup by Ann McGovern